MY LIFE WITH LURCHERS

MY LIFE
WITH
LURCHERS

DAVID HANCOCK

COCH-Y-BONDDU BOOKS

First published by Huddlesford Publications in 1987
This edition Coch-y-Bonddu Books 2005
© 1987 David Hancock
All rights reserved

ISBN 978-1-904784-07-4
ISBN 1-904784-07-0

Published & distributed by
COCH-Y-BONDDU BOOKS
MACHYNLLETH, POWYS, SY20 8DJ

01654 702837   www.anglebooks.com

Printed in Great Britain by
St Edmundsbury Press Ltd
Bury St Edmunds, Suffolk

Contents

—1—

Early Days

I T WOULD PERHAPS be poetic and comforting to the reader to say that I was born into a family of lurcher breeders and came from a long line of dog and lurcher experts, one of my forebears claiming to be the bane of such and such a gamekeeper, or possibly that my remote ancestors, remote enough to be respectable that is (just as most Americans like to add a little Indian blood to their own pedigrees providing it is sufficiently far back not to merit their own children being referred to as papooses), were from gypsy stock. Well, if this is the case I'm afraid the reader is in for a disappointment. I was born 55 years ago in a very middle class area of Sutton Coldfield, to a family of poultry farmers who intensively farmed a four-acre patch of battery houses, deep litter pens and chick barns, and the nearest we ever came to gypsies was to find their caravans occasionally blocking the lane down to the farm, or maybe now and again popping in to buy eggs or the odd worn out battery hen to be used as a boiling fowl to go into the camp cooking pot.

In the wartime years, and in the years immediately following the war, we trap-nested (to ascertain which of the hens were the best layers) and bred our own poultry, hatching a variety of popular crosses such as Black Leghorn × Rhode Island Red or White Leghorn × Rhode or the less prolific but larger birds such as Rhode × Sussex birds which laid a reasonable number of eggs and gave fairly large carcasses at the end of their laying life. Genetics was learned the hard way, not through lessons at King Edward's Grammar School which I attended, though I suppose my knowledge of Mendel's Law has stood me in good stead in my lurcher breeding days. For Pete's sake don't imagine every lurcher breeder goes head over heels for genetic breeding programmes and I'm the first to admit that a good many first-rate lurchers are the result of hit and miss tactics, but if one is going to be a top-rate breeder

Our four acre patch of battery houses.

of any form of livestock, be it poultry, white mice or dogs, then one has to know the genetic make-up of one's stock – and sadly a whole lot more about the diseases which can and eventually will plague that stock, but more of that depressing subject later.

We bred and reared our own turkeys in those days – massive broad-breasted bronze birds (giant replicas of the American wild turkey) which grew so large that not only did their legs collapse under them, but they were far too big for the average family and more suitable for the hotel trade. Some of the stags were so big they damaged the hens as they mated them and rearing batches of these stupid birds was such a problem that a loud bang or a low-flying aeroplane would cause the whole stupid brood to pile on top of each other and suffocate the bottom most. Birds are lighter these days but the temperament is just about the same. During the wartime years and after meat rationing made the theft of turkeys, chickens and even ducks for that matter, a highly profitable business, and there were always watch-dogs a plenty around the farm kept free, gratis and for nothing on the broken fowl waste and heads, food which incidentally was also boiled up with restaurant waste and fed to pigs. Pigs which grew to a size which would be unprofitable now that concentrates are available. We'd need a special licence to feed such fare today but in those days any who had the space, time and energy to produce food was encouraged to do so and curiously foot and mouth disease and the now common swine vesicular disease was practically unknown. What is amazing in the light of modern farming methods, improved management and specially bred livestock, is that we made a profit – but we did and lived a life of Riley on the food we produced, for we grew our own vegetables fertilised with natural muck and were literally self-sufficient.

Ducks were highly profitable livestock in those days. We kept Aylesburys – proper Aylesburys, not the fast fattening so called Aylesburys of today which are really Pekin and Aylesbury hybrids, but the real McCoy birds, slower to grow, but making large and heavy carcasses. However, ducks are hellers to attract rats, so we were seldom without several terriers running around the farm, a mix of Jack Russell and other breeds, and later, much later, a strain of Cairn terrier bred from Mrs Mawson's stock which ratted with the best of them. Funnily enough, although most authorities claim that the working instinct has been bred out of Cairns, the ones we kept until a matter of a few years ago, when through a misjudgement or oversight we let them die out, were fiery little beasts capable and more than willing to take on the most aggressive large dog, and with hunting instinct enough to put the majority of border terriers to shame. Dogs from this strain also went to ground naturally, but we kept them as ratters.

My parents were not particularly keen to have lurches, longdogs and the like on the farm. Greyhounds and even the fragile whippets had a reputation of being stock-worriers, and a greyhound on the rampage can very quickly see off an entire year's work in chicken rearing, or put paid to a batch of turkeys just by chasing them. Lurchers were also a little out of the question as the only sort of people who kept this type of dog – and a 'type' of lurcher existed in the Midlands during the war years, a type which bred almost true and was a far cry from the mish-mash one sees at lurcher shows today – were tinkers, gypsies and poachers who were carefully supervised by the police force in our rather rural and perhaps a little snooty area. It's curious to use the term 'rural area' to describe a fairly heavily built-up area like Sutton Coldfield, but in the wartime years, and in the days which immediately preceded the post-war building boom, Sutton Coldfield and Blade Street – a district rather than what the name implies – held a staggering quantity of game, and rabbits were abundant.

I kept spaniels, retrievers and a variety of gun dogs as a boy, and as soon as school finished and farm chores were completed I was off with dog and gun, hunting just about every type of game available. Pigeons were favourite quarry and despite the savage persecution given to these birds during wartime years, when war was literally declared on the ring-dove and any allied grain-eating species, as soon as the process of exterminating these birds was relaxed even slightly, the numbers literally shot up, and in 1948 the Midlands saw a plague of these birds. Funnily enough, in spite of the meat shortage it was nearly impossible to sell pigeons in those years, possibly due to the most misunderstood of Midlands sayings that 'three pigeons will kill a man', a saying which came about because unless a pigeon is cooked properly and for a very long time, it is tough and indigestible. Believe me, the saying has nothing to do with the supposed toxic nature of pigeon flesh. I've eaten hundreds and I've never been ill in my life – I've never even had a headache in fact.

Funnily enough, 1948 saw the purchase of my first lurcher puppy – a strictly 'pedigree unknown' beast bought as a whim I suppose from Lichfield livestock market when, in those days, dogs could be offered for sale in those wire cages which now harbour fancy poultry and worn out battery fowl. Markets of this nature were always supervised by RSPCA officials both uniformed and incognito for a dog could be purchased so cheaply that many inhuman types bought a dog – a once beloved pet of some family who could no longer control or afford the dog, or the seven and sixpence licence and wished to find it a good home – only to take the collar from the dog and turn the wretched creature loose. Thank God the RSPCA stopped this trade, though I was saddened to learn recently that there was an auction of dogs in South Wales and one lurcher was purchased simply for its collar and slip and then disposed of by the heartless purchaser. It's an unpleasant world by the sound of it, and I often wonder what happens to the dogs I breed when they have outlived their usefulness or the owners have become bored or maybe disenchanted with their dog. I tattoo the ears of my dogs these days, and endeavour to check on the fate of most of them. I hasten to add I don't sell a replacement to one of the chop-and-change merchants who change dogs more frequently than they change their socks, one week buying a puppy and then swopping it for another lurcher – and there are plenty of these in the lurcher world.

To hazard a guess at the breeding of my first lurcher would be a bit foolish to say the least. Ifi grew to perhaps 22″ at the shoulder, had a greyhoundy shape, a slape coat and could have been a mixture of collie, greyhound and probably a dash of street accident thrown in for good measure. Ifi looked sufficiently lurchery at twelve weeks, when I bought him, to cause my family a little dismay but he settled in to farm life after giving the fowl a chase or so just to show he was at least part sight hound, and became a fairly amicable farm pet. If there had been

time perhaps he'd have made an excellent hunting dog for in those days
the lurcher hadn't been ruined by mixtures of deerhound, saluki and
God knows what other exotic breeds non-thinking breeders have added
to the type. As it was there wasn't time to train him and he became a
self-taught hunter, returning home with whatever he caught and was
not really too fussy about where he went to catch it.

The poultry trade had begun to blossom after the war and my father
and I expanded the business, and so busy were we that lurchers, or dogs
of any breed for that matter, were the very last thing on our minds. We
worked the clock around, fell asleep and started work as soon as we
awoke. I've often envied the life of nine to five workers who literally
finish work on the bell, for the life of a farmer, or a stock breeder of any
sort for that matter, is a full time job and breaks and holidays are fitted
in as and when they can be. I think it was George Bernard Shaw who
said, 'Man has become a slave to the animals he has sought to enslave',
and only a stock keeper can realise the truth in that statement. Well,
one day my lurcher disappeared and for a while we didn't worry too
much as he was a love-lorn beast prone to take off for days when the
enticing odour of an in-season bitch wafted across to our farm, but after
a week or so we realised that all was not well. He never returned and
while I would like to think he was picked up by some poacher who made
good use of the dog's talents, in my heart of hearts I think I know what
happened to him. By his third year he had become a well known local
nuisance, a ransacker of dustbins, a thief of food and a bit of a pest on
the nearby shoots breaking into pheasant rearing pens, stealing poults,
putting up rabbits and the odd hare and causing my family to wince
each time there was a knock on the door. To kennel him, to chain him
up after two years of absolute freedom, would have been inhuman and
my bet is that he finished his life through a barrel of number five shot
and was secretly buried under a hedge on one of the nearby shoots. A
hell of a way to die? I don't think so. Ifi was the sort of dog whose life
consisted of taking chances and he'd run the gauntlet of gamekeepers
and enraged housewives for a fair old time – perhaps he was stolen and
maybe he did die a fireside death in some poacher's kitchen but I've
never been a romantic, anyway every stock breeder soon learns to face
up to reality or go quickly insane with the problems which attend the
keeping of any livestock.

I suppose I ran a little wild until comparatively late in life, hunting
and indulging in my passion for photography until I was 30 before
deciding to settle down to marriage. At that time the poultry trade was
fairly prosperous and there was no hint or foreboding of the bad days
which were to come. Egg and poultry meat production had reached an
all time high, and stock feed was at an all time cheap rate due to bumper

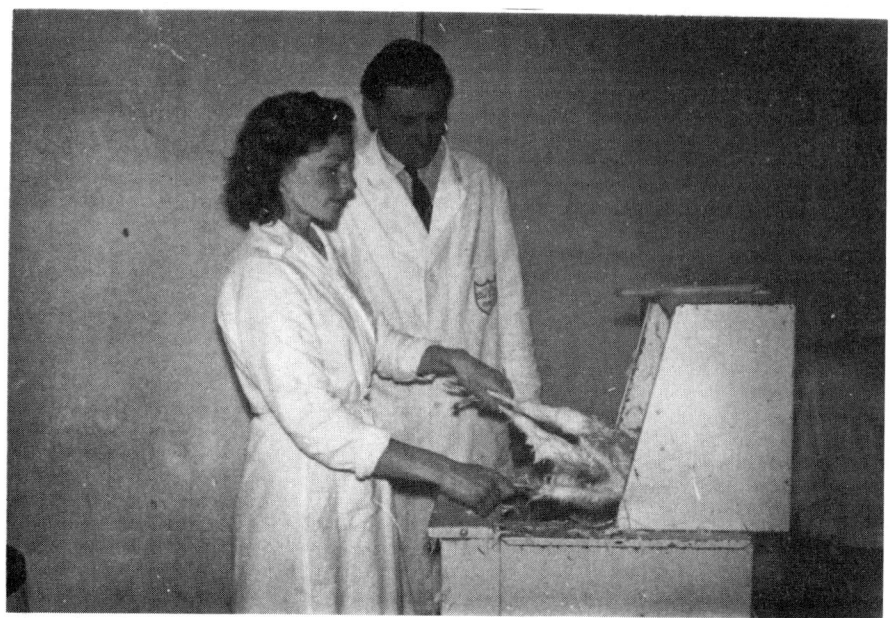

My wife Joan, plucking turkeys, before we were married.

crops of maize in the USA and a surfeit of fish meal high-grade protein. Sales increased dramatically and we increased our stock well aware (well, fairly aware) of the problems which could and did attend intensive farming.

I married Joan Bicknell who worked as a helper on our holding, and was the daughter of what can only be described as a local character. Joan's dad was a law unto himself, not giving a damn for anyone and caring even less about what people thought of him. He was an inveterate poacher and in the wartime years when rabbits fetched as much as five shillings apiece he must have poached half of Staffordshire, making Joan place nets and administering quite savage punishment if a rabbit escaped the folds of the purse net when he considered it was her fault. He had developed the art of escape to perfection when his escapades were detected and made good his get away by an ingenious device. When pursued by police, gamekeepers or irate farmers he escaped on a motor bike, a primitive antique affair with James Bond type equipment and when his pursuers gained on him he simply switched from petrol to a fume and smoke-making mix of oil, paraffin and petrol, creating clouds of smoke which blinded his pursuers, allowing him to escape and switch back to a normal mix. His carburettor probably suffered as did the rest of his ramshackle bike but he was never apprehended – an ingenious chap by any standards and one who would and did put to shame Frederick Rolfe, self-styled king of the Norfolk poachers.

Joan's father. A likeable old rogue.

Curiously Cyril and John Bicknell, his sons, after having learned this trade from their wayward father turned to the other side of the fence and became highly respected gamekeepers and foresters in Shropshire – making first-rate jobs of catching poachers. Set a thief to catch a thief.

Well, set a thief's son seems more apt under the circumstances perhaps. Cyril and John have proved priceless in obtaining hunting land for us and places where I can photograph lamping scenes – the most difficult action shots to photograph.

Joan with her brother Cyril Bicknell, a Shropshire gamekeeper.

Joan took to commercial dog breeding like a duck to water, inheriting so to speak, a ready-made kennel of German shepherd dogs and one or two Yorkshire terriers, diminutive beasts from which Joan selected large powerful bitches, mating them to very small stud dogs and providing self-whelping litters – a bit of a novelty amongst Yorkshire terrier litters these days I'm afraid, where a great many are born through forceps delivery or Caesarian sections. Good luck – well maybe, but Joan somehow inherited that peculiar indefinable quality known as 'stockmanship' a quality which somehow enables two people to buy identical stock, keep them under identical situations, feed identical foods and yet for some reason one breeder makes a success of his venture whilst the other becomes beset with a hundred or so problems and promptly goes broke. Two of our children, Sally and Thomas, have

Joan has always had an interest in dogs, even as a child.

15

inherited Joan's knack, technique, call it what you will, of stockmanship, but Peter – our middle child – has shown little interest in dogs and has become a car and motor bike freak.

Not all of Joan's ventures paid off however, though in some ways I learned much from Joan's most traumatic failure. Prompted by incredibly beautiful statues of Diana of the Chase plus dogs, and the fact that a film starring Judy Garland and Fred Astaire had given a new lease of life to borzoi sales, Joan invested in some Russian wolfhounds, huge elegant 34″ high beasts, which would have been more at home in a palace in St Petersburg than in a back yard of a poultry farm. Once the romance of their incredible beauty – and by God they were beautiful – had begun to wear a bit thin, various other defects began to manifest themselves. Firstly, I noticed that the spindly limbs were far too fragile and that a course over the rough plough behind the farm invariably rendered them 'hors de combat' for weeks, scarcely able to totter let alone run. Yet there was no denying that they'd chase anything that moved. For a while I believed that the specimens Joan had obtained had defective hearing, for they refused to respond to command, and simply wandered around the farm aimlessly, uncaring of the oaths and shrieks I uttered to get them into their kennels at night. Convinced we had defective stock I consulted other breeders of borzois, who seemed amused at my ignorance and assured me that there was nothing unusual about the strain Joan was keeping. Fortunately, and I say this rather reservedly as Joan liked the borzois, one day all three decided not to come back and promptly disappeared from our premises never to be seen again. This incident taught me quite a lot about borzois in particular, and sight hound disposition in general, and I started to have ideas which were to be put to good use when I eventually became a full time lurcher breeder.

Curiously, I became a professional lurcher breeder by the merest chance, and partly because my wife kept goats. I think I'd best explain this fairly quickly before the reader puts down the book and starts thinking that I am raving bats. Joan had bought a few pedigree goats of the Sanaan breed, white goats typical of the type found tethered at every roadside croft from Land's End to John O'Groats. They were top quality stock and mated to a top class sire they began to produce very showy kids. Joan boxed up a few and started taking them to minor agricultural shows where she had some reasonable degree of success. At Alrewas near Lichfield, she showed a particularly classy kid and was approached by an astoundingly attractive girl of about 21 and her man friend, a gaunt rather tatty-looking man of about 33, with whom the girl was living. The girl spoke with the typical lucidly clear accent of a young woman who had attended a top-grade private school, but the man, who behaved very oddly working out a mathematical formula concerning the incidence of hip dysplacia in golden retrievers, seemed rather lost in his world of facts and figures. The girl excused her companion's attitude and his reluctance to speak succinctly. 'Don't mind him, he's convinced God is a mathematician and is such a sceptic that he does not believe he's been to the toilet unless he has weighed himself.' She stroked Joan's goat and asked a hundred pertinent questions about goats and goat breeds while her donkey-coated companion returned to the pair uttering something like 3.654, or some other figure that seemed totally unintelligible to both Joan and the girl. The girl introduced herself as Elizabeth McKenna and her male friend as Brian Plummer.

—2—

Plummer and the Experiments in Lurcher Breeding

THE PAIR CAME back to our house for tea with Joan, and I have been firm friends with Plummer ever since – well, as much of a friend as one can be with a person of Plummer's disposition. At that time he had just come out of what can best be described as a rather peculiar patch in his life, a time when he had given up his job, refused dole and had attempted a rather devastating spell of self-sufficiency. The spell had left him physically damaged and also, while this is almost certain to hurt, rather mentally ill. Few people know the real reasons for his need to opt out of teaching or society for that matter, but the truth is he is naturally solitary, very ill at ease with people and also what is known as a lateral thinker. His scientific articles of some 20 years ago were treated with disdain and perhaps a hint of amusement at the time – though now some of his articles are generally accepted by the scientific fraternity – and the flak he took from science writers finally toppled the balance and made him opt out. He is perhaps an ultra-sensitive person, far too easily hurt by criticism, and avoids country shows because he cannot take the barracking certain well known idiots give him. I take this irritation in my stride, but Plummer simple folds into himself after such people try to upset him, and frankly he is ill-designed to live in a world populated by people. The depressive spells he hints at in his books are far more severe then one can imagine and last for weeks, until Joan or I visit him to get him to snap out of these bouts, and frankly he is impossible to live with as a variety of women have found out to their cost. The ridge between a high level of IQ and mental illness is easily crossed and I feel Plummer has made the crossing to and fro several times in the spell we have known him.

Lest I should seem totally critical of a man who I claim as a friend, it should be pointed out that he has several good qualities to compensate for his peculiarities. He is unmistakably articulate when he decides he

Brian Plummer in deep trance-like thought.

should talk to people, speaks several languages fluently and has an abnormal general knowledge. He is a workaholic, capable of working non-stop without sleep for spells of up to four days – thereby fulfilling my wife's prediction that he is a candidate for a possibly fatal coronary – and eats when the mood takes him sometimes going seven or eight days without food when he is working on a book or a problem. Another peculiarity which characterises this strange man is that when faced with a seemingly insolvable problem he puts himself into a trance-like sleep to work out a solution or evolve an idea and wakes when the solution has become obvious to him. I have seen this trance-like sleep take place in his house, in cafes and more particularly on motor journeys, when he will suddenly pull over, ask me to drive and within seconds put himself into a catatonic trance from which it is impossible to waken him until he has worked out the matter which is troubling him. His memory is phenomenal and after reading a book in any of the languages he speaks, he is able to write the book word for word even a year afterwards. His intellect is without question, his money sense is lamentable and he is totally incapable of realising whether he is in debt or affluent. As I have said he is totally impossible to live with, and very difficult to understand. Liz had brought him out of his weird world with a vengeance and had left her all mod cons house in Rugeley to live in his half-completed cottage, the roof of which was at that time covered in a series of tarpaulins which steamed in summer and dripped icy rain in winter. She would have been a steadying influence on his wildly erratic life and had she stayed she would have prevented the massive depressive bouts which followed in the next 15 years. However, she was unable to tolerate the desperate depressions and the series of amorous adventures which ran hand in hand with his life, and one day she quietly slipped out of Plummer's life leaving him to return to his chaotic existence.

During his spell of opting out he corresponded frequently with scientists such as Lorenz, Dobzansky, Zenner and even the much abused Emanuel Velikovsky and strangely these pillars of the scientific world seemed to accept his lateral thinking. However, when he returned to teaching, the staff instantly labelled him 'peculiar', rejecting him, accusing him and generally making his life a misery. One incident that sticks out about this time is when the schools in the area where Plummer taught staged an inter-school staff quiz on general knowledge. One day Plummer turned up to compete to find the rest of his staff hadn't. To complete the round he played the entire staff of the opposing school and won easily, but went into a wildly depressive bout shortly afterwards and never again competed in those contests. As I have mentioned and I'll say it again, he is not suited to live in a world populated by people.

At the time we met him he bred a very typey strain of lurcher, slape-coated and with obvious collie blood that he bred by mating half-brother to half-sister. About five years before he had introduced greyhound blood – neat greyhound blood at that, and while he had kept the type of dog he bred, he had lost nose sensitivity, ability and sagacity just to obtain speed and was desperately trying to revive the strain he had kept since he was 12 obtaining his first puppy from a man called James Archigho – a Romany tinker Plummer had read about in Brian Vesey Fitzgerald's *It's My Delight*. The original stock would have resembled brindle editions of Wooley Bear or Red Wiggler, the collie-type lurcher seen in the *1982 Hunter's Year Book*, but by an ill-advised cross with a greyhound, a half-brother of which was Irish Airport, he bred a sleeker more greyhoundy strain which looked the part but were certainly not up to the standard of the old strain. Since then repeated collie crosses have revived the strain somewhat but that is perhaps a story which is a little out of context.

During the year preceding the time Plummer met my wife he reluctantly returned to teaching, hating every minute of it. To break the

Wooley Bear.

monotony of the life he started a rather ghoulish science club after school, dissecting various animals at first and finally specialising in cast greyhounds which had been put down once their useful days were over. At first his science club consisted of some five children aged 16, two of whom became biologists, and a further pair doctors, and all of whom attributed their interest in anatomy to the dissection lessons given by Plummer. He became fairly convinced that by carefully weighing running muscle, heart, lungs and liver he could determine what actually made a champion and recorded with his usual maddening accuracy the weights of organs and muscles of failures and track champions, but failed to come to a conclusion apart from an unproven theory that the difference between a track champion and an 'also ran' was that the champion was possessed of a greater ability to go through the pain barrier which must plague a dog towards the end of a race. He wrote a scientific paper entitled *The Pain Barrier* but it received little recognition apart from a letter or so from some scientists in Bar Harbour, Maine, questioning his results, and as the science class had grown to over 50 the dissection of dogs caused considerable dismay among the rest of the staff who appealed to the headmaster to stop these ghastly experiments.

Frankly the cessation of this science club proved a sad loss to the children, though in fairness the experiments proved nothing and certainly did not prove of any scientific value to greyhound racing or lurcher breeding.

That year he obtained three greyhound bitches free of charge and began to experiment on breeding a variety of lurchers and longdogs, crossing his greyhounds with a variety of exotic and often unsuitable sires, and as he was plagued by thefts the lot of rearing the whelps and socialising them fell to Joan and myself and this more than any other event set me on the course to breeding the strains of lurcher I breed today. A variety of first cross hybrids were produced, reared by us, given away by Plummer to certain people who promised not to sell them, and keep accurate records, only to break their promises nine times out of ten as soon as an offer of money was forthcoming. Some of the stock looked spectacular. One litter reared by Joan out of a Solar Prince sister mated to an Ardkinglas deerhound produced magnificent beasts, one of which is still owned by Terry Aherne of Tamworth. Bitches from this litter were pictures and were outstandingly beautiful and fast. The males were larger, less nimble and not particularly well proportioned. They influenced the lurcher scene in Britain tremendously but not one had a modicum of brains in its head, though they jumped well and could with considerable effort be taught to retrieve in a half-hearted fashion.

The bull terrier hybrids were oddly enough a lot more level in type and more biddable and far more useful all round dogs, though I have always found that the type of person who is keen to work at training a dog determines the end product as much as the breeding of the lurcher. Plummer used a son of an elderly dog called The Black Monarch, owned by Boam and Barker, and the leggy, terrier-like shape of the dog perhaps contributed to the shape of the lurcher progeny. I believe two families of lurchers still carry some of this blood, but the results were far from satisfactory, though several grandchildren, the result of mating their first cross hybrids to greyhounds, did fairly well on 'down market' flapping tracks even run against pure greyhounds. Altogether neither Joan nor I found the type to be of any value as working dogs and stories of kennel fights concerning these dogs were fairly common. Certainly Plummer's experiments were based on the work of Lord Orford who crossed bulldogs with greyhounds to get guts and stamina into his strain and the first Waterloo Cup winner had a dash of bulldog blood. Plummer had far less success.

Other crosses were tried with varying degrees of success and included hydrids between Irish terriers sired by an unregistered dog from Whittington Barracks, a Rillington Bedlington terrier which bred a very level litter, all of which proved poor doers in later life for some obscure reason or other, and even an abortive try at a hybrid twixt an imported saluki and a fairly well-bred greyhound. The progeny were fast, elegant, full of stamina, scatty, and habitual sheep worriers, and some of the tales which could be told of this litter should be best left out of a book of this nature.

The majority of these experiments at matings proved little short of disastrous, and contributed greatly to the decline of the standard of the lurcher throughout the country as the majority were bred from and often as not mated to unsuitable sires. Brian is the first to admit to the damage he did.

Light at the end of the tunnel appeared in 1971 when Plummer began experimenting with collie/greyhound hybrids. His first trial being twixt a Scottish bearded collie and a pale blue Irish Airport bitch. The progeny were black-blue and one was a tawny brindle, which he gave to David James of Bloxwich, who was breeding collie lurchers from border collies, and who found the bearded puppy not as biddable as a border counterpart. He was also a sheep worrier and went the way of all lurchers who show this disposition. Plummer placed the majority in Durham where a close friend, the barrister John Winch lived, and apart from one or two unhappy accidents the litter was a great success. One, a bitch with a damaged leg ligament, was to become a famous brood, though her progeny did better in the showing than in the working field as Smith repeatedly mated her to the Ardkinglas deerhound/ greyhound cross Plummer had given Terry Aherne, not a mating I would advise. However, the results obtained from this litter were heartening and considerably better than those of the whelps obtained by other matings, and he continued with his experiments using the same dog. All in all Plummer's experiments and the puppies produced by them may have been a source of entertainment to the amateur hunter who worked their crosses but they did irreparable harm to the lurcher scene. The whole mish-mash were not considered an end in themselves as I'm sure their creator intended them to be, but were mated with each other by undiscerning breeders who produced stock ranging from typey track greyhounds to a set of monsters which had characteristics of bull terriers, deerhounds, Irish terriers and Kerry Blue terriers. If I reflect on those times the Midland lurcher scene was indeed a mess and perhaps I began breeding at the most fortuitous time in the history of the lurcher, when a mad mix up was just beginning to level out to a substandard type which was perhaps only as useful as a second grade greyhound.

The coursing bug, the desire to chase hares which is the prerogative of the greyhound or the saluki, rather than the lurcher, was also at its peak at this time and while Plummer was desperately trying and equally desperately failing to produce his wonder dog, the rest of the lurcher world were simply mating greyhounds or salukis to their lurchers to produce coursing dogs. At this point I feel it only fair to declare that I have never produced a lurcher that was the equal of a first-rate top class coursing greyhound at the sport of knocking down hares, nor has it been my intention, and when I am asked for a hare coursing dog pure and simple I advise them to buy a greyhound, preferably from the Linden Eland line which I rate highly as catch dogs as much as conventional coursing dogs, and if not a greyhound then a good strain of coursing saluki. Perhaps at this point I should add that I am reluctant to allow my three quarter bred collie lurchers to mate pure greyhounds to breed the very fashionable seven-eighth greyhound/one-eighth collies which find a ready market in Cheshire, Lancashire and in parts of Yorkshire. Far too much greyhound blood has already been added to the conventional lurcher and a three quarter bred is diluted enough for anyone. Any person wanting a dog with more speed shouldn't countenance a lurcher but go for a longdog or better still a pure bred greyhound.

However, it would be unfair and certainly most unreasonable of me to simply cast off all Plummer's experiments in lurcher breeding though as I pointed out in recent *Shooting Times* articles, dogs bred from greyhound mated to bull, Irish or Kerry terriers no more qualify for the title lurcher than does the deerhound/greyhound hybrid. Perhaps the most interesting hybrids were his bearded collie greyhounds which have been mentioned earlier in this chapter and have excelled as lamp dogs in Durham. The recalcitrant nature of the cross – it was difficult to control, hard to lead train (but when really trained unbeatable as a lamp dog) – had prompted Plummer to experiment still further in the field of true lurchers and thus Merle was bred for him by the unfortunate Dai Fish or South Wales by mating a blue merle border collie to what Plummer calls, rather unfairly, an indifferent track greyhound. In point of fact the greyhound was far from indifferent despite the fact that during its active life it was used for flapping, coursing over very rough country and fox catching. The dog was in fact a son of Sandstar, a Derby-winning dog and a grandson of Solar Prince, a line highly prized by lurcher breeders as a source of course, catch, kill and carry dogs. However, more on this rather peculiar stud lurcher later for he featured heavily in my own lurcher breeding programme.

A more interesting cross is not mentioned by Plummer for some reason though it was to have a very far-reaching effect on the breeding of the modern lurcher than the hybrid bred by Dai Fish. Plummer obtained on indefinite loan a bitch collie, blue merle in colour and a

Merle.

trifle heavy for my own liking, from a Welsh hill farmer called David Jones, a common enough name and a common enough type of dog for she was straight working bred, sired by an unregistered hill collie male out of a blue merle bitch whose grandfather had won in minor field trials in mid-Wales. It was scarcely an impressive pedigree, not on paper that is, but she was free from collie eye anomaly which plagues many strains of trial collie and also completely steady in every way. Proof of this steady disposition was displayed on the day after he brought her to the Midlands. She was a little touchy about the change of ownership and subsequently he kept her in his van, a dirty Ford Escort which was seldom washed and never polished, across the dust of which some wag had written 'disgusting' which remained on the van for two years until Plummer gave the vehicle to Moses Smith. The bitch remained in the van for two days and when Plummer attended a bonfire party staged by one of his innumerable Godchildren in Walsall, the bitch slept through the entire din. It would have been difficult to find steadier foundation stock for any strain, but the strain had defects which were later to manifest themselves in no uncertain manner.

To test the produce of this bitch, Plummer who was once again plagued by thefts, sent the bitch to a railway worker called Paul Taylor, who lived near Melton Mowbray and whose photograph appeared on the front cover of *Diary of a Hunter*. Taylor selected two studs to use on her, a Solar Prince grandson now greatly valued by Plummer as lurcher

25

foundation stock, and a blue and white open race dog with strong lines to Silver Hope, the sire of Patricia's Hope, winner of the English, Welsh and Scottish Derbies in 1972 and the English Derby of 1973 after he had spent a year at stud and had made a comeback to sweep the board. The stud dog was not favoured by Plummer who had little faith in the line, but the greyhound proved a willing stud dog and bred Taylor a litter of 11 puppies which were perhaps the most variable litter I have ever seen, though as predicted they were either black or merle in colour. Taylor kept one which he called Fleet, a misnomer as he was a cloddy beast of a type which was more suited as a stud to mate greyhounds to breed three quarter breds than as an all round work dog. I have never produced a half bred as heavy as this dog though there are lamp dogs of this size and shape that are reputedly some of the best in the country catching 50 rabbits a night with ease and scarcely blowing after the effort. Another puppy which went to Guy Page, a mental hospital nurse in Birmingham, spent ages trapping rabbits with its feet – a curious collie trait – before he mastered the art of picking up properly. However, a fine-boned bitch went south to Suffolk to a coursing enthusiast called Porter who entered her carefully and took his time over starting her to hare. His patience paid off and she became a famous hare dog perhaps one of the fastest half breds of her day, winning against longdog and cast greyhound until she died of injuries at the age of six. Porter tried repeatedly to get an identical replacement, but the odds on producing a replica were very small, so the mating was never repeated. Another puppy went to the Jacksons of Nottingham, a dun merle bitch with an ugly shape who might have proved a useful brood, but was an indifferent courser and not a particularly good all round dog. Jackson, who at that time made nets for CTF and also Kings, never continued the bloodline and I believe no progeny were bred from the litter. At three weeks old the puppies were enormous and the peculiarities of the strain of collies began to manifest themselves for the bitch went down with milk fever and needed daily injections of calcium boroglutinate even after the puppies were weaned. It was a warning shot which fortunately Plummer recognised and to a certain extent curbed and once again I shall qualify the expression 'to a certain extent'.

The bearded collie line used to create Moses Smith's bitch Steel, and the sheep worrier owned by David James, was a good true breeding working line free from border collie outcrosses and very few working beardie strains are true breeding. They bred large litters were very hardy and were bred by an Englishman called Mike Broadridge who had been exiled to Scotland but had a phenomenal knowledge of the bearded collie as a worker if not as a show dog. His stock was rangy and as free from genetic fault as possible, working hard day in day out,

Guy Page with Jude.

self-whelping and reputedly had one of the best food conversion rates in any strain. Milk fever was unknown and they were also quite biddable and above all early starters, which I shall explain in my later chapter on collies. Plummer returned the border collie bitch to the Broadridge dog and mated him for the following reasons: firstly, the line from Broadridge was very true breeding; secondly, they were free from foot injury; and thirdly, they had very thick coats and hard leathery hides beneath the fur. The merle border collie bitch lent a steady disposition to the stock and a remarkable herding instinct inherited from Jones' stock.

27

The resulting litter were 12 in number and all resemble either Polish sheepdogs or early Welsh Greys of the sort seen in drovers' photographs. Once again the bitch obliged by going down with milk fever and the litter was reared by hand.

Parvo virus hit at that time and Plummer lost half the litter, which were already weakened by being hand-reared. One bitch puppy was given to Gerald Barlow, a farmer who keeps cattle in Huddlesford, and has proved an excellent worker though a little peculiar as she has a decided hatred for one of Barlow's cattle, and at rounding up time prior to milking she tears into this one cow furiously. Another puppy from this litter became ill and was treated by a Lichfield veterinary surgeon, Richard Jones, and promptly received its saviour's name Richard. The dog was to prove perhaps the most important sire in the pedigree of the modern collie lurcher.

Sally – now known as Old Sally.

However, the collie is only one side of a lurcher family and the greyhound side is just as important. At that time Plummer had seen Bauhus run and examined the dog in detail. Shapewise this son of Solar Prince was perhaps the most perfect of greyhounds, incorporating the shape and quality of Newdown Heather with the substance of hard leg drive of Cotton King. His potential as a sire became manifest when he bred not only One and Only and the Derby winner Sand Star, but also when he produced Letesia, the dam of both Minnesota Miller and Minnesota Yank, both of whom scored in successive years in the Waterloo Cup. Plummer enthused over the dog with near mania and decided (after much calculation) to buy a stock from the dog to start a lurcher strain. Sadly Bauhus' worth was also sensed by the Americans who bought the dog which bred a succession of winners in the States and was as great a loss to British bloodstock as the theft of Shergar. Later Plummer dropped lucky, or rather unlucky, as he located a Bauhus granddaughter. Sadly she had a shattered pelvis and was a non-starter as a breeder and recklessly Plummer plunged himself into debt to buy her sister, a bitch whose kennel name was Sally. I use the word recklessly in an ill-advised sense for Sally became unquestionably the greatest lurcher breeding greyhound of her age, and this I believe brings Plummer's part in the creation of the strain I breed to an end, and despite the gentle fun I have made of his eccentricities, the comments I have written have been absolutely truthful and in no way meant to hurt this absurdly over-sensitive friend.

—3—

Meanwhile Down on the Farm

A FEW YEARS AGO Ted Moult who not only advertised Everest double glazing but also farmed a fairly large tract of land at Swadlincote near Derby, and who had a dazzling intelligence despite his rustic accent, spoke in a debate with one of the Friends of the Earth type groups who were not only against chemical fertilisation of the soil but also against intensive farming. By intensive farming I mean battery house pullets, broiler bird houses, rabbit farming and veal calf raising. Moult heard out his critics patiently and then capped the situation succinctly with one crushing statement explaining that at the present time two-thirds of the earth's population were undernourished, but without intensive farming, the use of chemical fertilisers and equally dangerous and toxic weed sprays and insecticides, the rest of us would join the other two-thirds in the famine stakes. Make no bones about it, organically grown foods may or may not be healthier and free range eggs from foul allowed to wander freely to pick up insects might be more nutritious (in point of fact science has proven they are not and no taste test has ever confirmed that even seasoned gourmets are capable of detecting the difference between free-range and battery laid eggs), the fact remains that to produce enough food to feed the world and to keep the British farmer in business, 'unnatural' (if that's what organic enthusiasts want to call it) methods are here to stay.

I own four acres of land and have produced hundreds of tons of eggs, thousands of tons of broiler fowl, ducks and turkeys and perhaps half a million tons of bi-products, some of which are unmentionable, on a piece of land which if organically farmed and stocked with a small flock of happy clucking free-range pullets wouldn't pay the milk bill let alone keep my family alive. I am an intensive farmer, keeping as many broiler fowl in sheds as economics allow, keeping hens in battery pens, ducks in

Ducks by the thousands.

thousands in dark barns and turkeys in hundreds in sheds where they are kept in 24-hour daylight and never see a blade of grass.

I don't intend to go into an argument about the morals of such animal husbandry and point out that the correctly balanced diet these hens eat ensures better health than an insect-scratched meal and that if hens weren't happy in cages they wouldn't lay eggs anyway. I confess I dislike claustrophobic conditions myself but as I've mentioned there isn't any other way to make poultry pay, and having gone on for a page or so about the economics of poultry farming I'm going to confess I didn't make it pay either for in the end like hundreds of other poultry keepers I too had to close down.

Livestock kept under cover in intensive conditions thrive in a manner of speaking as they are spared the vagaries of the weather, but the forever warm, forever sunlit conditions of the battery or intensive farm also provide not only ideal conditions for livestock, but they are fairly pleasant places for bacteria and virus alike and once a disease breaks out in such places it can and often does spread like wildfire. I learned a series of simple rules about keeping livestock from my days as an intensive poultry farmer and I intend to stick to them. If a disease breaks out for God's sake don't pretend it hasn't, admit to it straight away, contact someone who knows about it and get the disease identified immediately. It the breeder does this he's in with a chance of controlling it, if not eradicating it, and if he can't eradicate it he must cull his entire stock, take the necessary methods of disinfection and

31

fumigation and give the disease a chance to die out before he starts up again.

A breeder of poultry or any sort of livestock for that matter, who refuses to admit that his stock are going down with a disease and keeps the vet or Ministry of Agriculture reps well away soon finds he's in a hell of a mess and has also infected half the country with his problems as well. The TV and the media generally get a lot of mileage out of photographs of heart-broken farmers bulldozing and cremating thousands of cattle in crater-like bonfires, and believe me I know it is a heart-breaking business, enough to make the hardest-hearted man burst into tears, but it's absolutely necessary and I've come to realise that the slaughter of thousands of apparently healthy birds and beasts to prevent a disease spreading is as much a part of farming as 'we plough the fields and scatter'.

Most livestock keepers have to learn to harden their hearts to disease outbreaks or simply go into another line of business. It's a tough game and as President Truman said, 'If you can't stand the heat, stay out of the kitchen', and believe me there's a hell of a lot of heat in the kitchen of intensive farming, and a lot of people leave the kitchen rather than face it. I openly admit that later I was to become one of those who left the said kitchen.

Like it or not the reader needs to know a spot of science to realise the problems my family and I faced during these days which embittered me so much I can't stand the sight of a chicken, or the stench of their ever-present ammonia-scented dung. Diseases are caused by two organisms, bacteria and viruses, known to the layman and early scientists from Pasteur to the twentieth-century scientists as germs. There's a hell of a lot of a difference between the two and thank God I learned all about them before I went into dog breeding. A bacterium is a large germ and most will succumb to a chemical organism called an antibiotic. So if a hen or such like gets a bacterial infection like *E. Coli*, an antibiotic added to the food will, providing the bird is not too far gone, stop the problem and get things back to normal. A virus is another kettle of fish. A million virus can live in a bacterium and they have an unnatural gift of recurring even after to all intents and purposes they are dead – the process is too complicated to explain, so I'll deliberately give it a miss. Antibiotics don't do a damn thing to viral infections though they do stop bacterial infections which follow in the wake of some virus. Virus breed at a hell of a rate and are so difficult to kill as to be a nightmare to control.

The art of stock keeping is transferable so to speak and the principles of poultry keeping apply equally to dog management. After each batch of poultry was removed from a pen – be they chicks, hens, turkeys or broilers – it was standard practice to steam clean the pen to remove all grime under which such a variety of bacterium and virus not only live but multiply. A wash down with a strong solution of hypochlorite, a substance a bit like Domestos, also helps do the trick and finally when all vents, gaps, door jambs *etc* are blocked tightly to make the place airtight, a pan of formaldehyde crystals heated on a gas fire, or if one wants to take the risk, mixed with potassium permanganate crystals, is used to fumigate the still wet buildings. Of course as soon as air rushes into the fumigated sheds it does bring in virus particles and the whole process starts up again. It does, however, give the fowl a breathing space to grow and come to a suitable age for killing or develop an immunity to the disease as the viral level of the premises increases. Even then, if one keeps poultry in number one must expect a relatively high mortality rate and the longer one keeps poultry on the premises then the greater the risk of infection and the greater the problem of fumigating and disinfecting the premises. Some farms are actually known to be 'turkey sick' – in other words have such a high microscopic bacterial climate fatal to turkeys that these birds can not be reared there. Sufficient to say my father had run the poultry farm since before my birth, and this may give just an indication of the problems a poultry keeper in my position had to encounter. I didn't go to university to learn virology – the subject was literally thrust at me as soon as I started farming and thank God it has served me well during my stint as a lurcher breeder. The treatment saw us over the deadly and baffling Marek's Infection, the various mixes of virus and bacillus that causes hens to lay soft-shelled eggs, and even Newcastle Disease, but to bore the reader with details of these diseases would be superfluous though it proved excellent training when I became a professional dog breeder.

In the 1960s the poultry trade boomed, eggs were reasonably priced and stock feed although not cheap was sufficiently inexpensive to allow the poultry breeder to survive if not flourish. White egg producing breeds bred from Leghorn crosses were no longer profitable as it was nearly impossible to sell white eggs for some stupid reason or other, but after a slight hiccup the poultry breeders came up with a brown egg layer which produced as many eggs as its white egg laying counterpart. All in all things looked reasonably rosy and while we weren't really prosperous we lived reasonably well. It was, however, a short-lived boom if boom it could be called. We kept in close touch with the Ministry of Agriculture, knew their vets and representatives on first name terms and when a few poultry farms went out of business we didn't. However, even at that time the writing was on the wall for the British egg and poutry meat producer.

Various changes began to make alterations to the British market.

There was a spate of publicity that eggs were rich in cholesterol, the substance which was then thought to cause heart disease, and egg consumption in the Western World dropped sharply for a number of years, particularly after Stillman, the get-thin-quickly American dietician doctor, advocated that no person should eat more than one egg a day if he had what Stillman described, a bit loosely perhaps, as cholesterol worries. Duck eggs, supposedly lower in cholesterol, underwent a popularity revival for a month or two after the publication of the book until the producers realised that ducks consumed one-and-seven-eighth times the amount of food as chickens to produce only a slightly larger number of eggs per year. Furthermore ducks will not respond to battery care and quickly turn even the best kept farm into a filthy quagmire in a matter of days. It was a temporary setback perhaps and the egg-eating public quickly went back to its normal diet regardless of Stillman and his cholesterol/heart attack propaganda. It was a knock,

Free-ranging Biros fighting at the Rare Breeds Trust.

however, that medium-sized egg producers like ourselves could ill afford.

Another minor hiccup occurred over the free-range vogue which caught on in the 1970s when certain people of a high moral calibre no doubt, but little economic sense, set up a campaign to boycott the sale of battery produced eggs claiming the yolks of free-range eggs were richer in colour than battery hen yolks – easily compensated for by adding a carotene additive to poultry meal. They neglected to mention that in free-foraging a hen or pullet burns up more energy hunting for insects and grubs than it gets from eating the creatures and that free-range poultry, like organically grown vegetables, are not economically viable. The craze gave a shot in the arm to the Rare Breeds Trust who were breeding old-fashioned fowl still capable of foraging but the fad soon came to an end when free-range producers realised the cost of producing 'naturally' laid eggs – that advertisement has always puzzled me. This craze too gave a temporary set back to the battery farmer but the big blow was yet to come.

Poultry food costs soared suddenly in the 1970s. British barley, wheat and other European grains went up sharply in price, but the price of maize, Indian corn, call it what you will, which is the corn on the cob grain produced in the millions of tons in America, rocketed. A bad harvest following the sharp increase sent poultry food prices to a level which could not be acceptable even to the very highly mechanised ultra-efficient poultry farms which were the envy of the world in the 1970s. Straight on top of the price increases, international fishing regulations caused the catches of fish to drop and the price of fish meal, the most expensive of high quality protein food, went sky-high. Soya, a naturally produced vegetable food high in protein but deficient in AOF vitamins, also went up in price and slowly poultry farm after poultry farm began to close, the smaller, more old-fashioned ones first but the large, more mechanised ones were quite close on their heels.

Plummer gives a gentle ending to his book, *Omega*, quite simply not to hurt the feelings of a friend, saying my farm was bought for housing development. It's time to tell the truth, Brian, and the truth is I went into liquidation without a clue how I was going to get out of the hellish mess the poultry business had put me in. I was over 50; labour, and young labour at that, was there for the begging and believe me things looked black.

It's at times like then when one really appreciates a family which pulls together and my family did just that. Joan, my wife, set up a market stall selling plants around the Midlands. Aubrey, who has lodged with us since he was a boy, set up a similar stall selling toilet goods and Sally, my eldest child, who had quit 'A' levels to help on the farm, promptly went out and in fierce competition obtained a good or at least a reasonable job. Peter, my son, became a tiler and Thomas, who was still in school, began to set up his own small firewood business. I wasn't given time to feel superfluous and set to making good old greenhouses – once used as places to grow exotic fruit to amuse if not feed the family and began market gardening, producing flowers and vegetable seedlings which Joan sold on her stall, or when things were tough, hawked around door to door like a gypsy. Some of our family ventures floundered a little perhaps. Pete bought plastic moulds to manufacture concrete garden ornaments and these weren't exactly successful, but what was more important was the whole family pulled together functioning as one unit and slowly but surely we began to haul ourselves upwards again, not to prosperity perhaps, we have never been prosperous, but at least we kept our heads above water and the gloom lifted just a little.

—4—

The Start of the Lurcher Stud

I HAD A fairly strict upbringing and was taught to accept gifts I did not want graciously, politely and not to offend the giver, but it was a hell of a temptation to look a gift-horse in the mouth when Plummer turned up in his mucky van and took out three in-season bitches. One, Sally, the Bauhus bred bitch I already knew. She had become a famous brood almost overnight when she had bred a litter of two puppies one of which became Eddie Jones' Celt – now arguably the most famous lurcher in the country and certainly the best known, and the other Hooten's Blue, a finely built pied dog, merle-patched and greyhoundy, which had a greater turn of speed than Celt and a more athletic disposition, but somehow lacked the robust stamina and constant good form of which Celt was famous. Plummer had been plagued by tinkers at the time he mated the bitch to his half bred merle collie/greyhound and put the bitch out to whelp at Michael's Kirby's place in Aldridge. Kirby was at that time one of Plummer's ratting team who sometimes ratted five nights a week at my farm and other places and was quite a dextrous catcher of rats.

He was no dog breeder, however, and when Sally whelped three days later in sharp, cold weather, Michael was caught unawares without a heat lamp, and with a maiden bitch, a bitch past her prime producing a litter. He lost three out of the five puppies and Plummer gave him the remaining two providing he kept an accurate record of where they went and what they did. That day Corporal Hooten phoned Plummer from Germany and booked the pied puppy. Three weeks later Eddie, a slow-speaking, highly articulate and down-to-earth education officer from Wolverhampton, a Welshman through and through, decided to retire and buy a lurcher as a 'pal'. He wanted a smallish dog for killing the odd rabbit or so. As luck would have it he bought a large white-collared black puppy, collie marked and with a hunting instinct so

Eddie Jones with Celt in October 1984 on the Isle of Man.

strong that it became Eddie's ticket to the world of lurchers. Celt, who was Eddie's first lurcher, was seldom equalled in the field and never beaten, and by the time Sally decided to come into season again both Celt and Blue were carving a name for themselves as hunting dogs and making fools out of established dogs which were supposedly unbeatable – a term I've since learned to avoid at all costs I must add.

Plummer presented the three bitches to me fairly calmly as if I had asked him for them. 'They will serve to breed you a top-grade kennel of lurchers', he added, parting with Sally a little sadly I thought at the time. 'The other two are sired by Derby winners and are closely related to Solar Prince', he added, as proof of their value, 'and mated to the right dog they will breed you as good a line as anything in the country.' The brother of his merle dog mated to a Solar Prince daughter had at that time bred a three quarter bred which had become a legendary catch dog killing seven out of seven at Lincoln and had changed hands for £3280 at Appleby that summer. The dog had the reputation of being as good as a shotgun as a provider of hares and even gypsies like George Gaskin who had seen the dog win, didn't consider the price too outlandish for a dog of this calibre and consistency. However, Merle was in his infancy as a stud. He was slow to mate and a reluctant sire until his retirement and I was fully aware that his litter to Sally could be a one swallow summer. Graciously, but I must admit reluctantly, I accepted

Sally and Simone soon after Plummer gave them to us.

the greyhounds without quite knowing why. I had owned, kept and bred lurchers but to imagine making a living from breeding them seemed a little far fetched at the time. Sally, my oldest child, was a little less gracious about the gifts. 'There are hundreds of ads for lurchers in every paper you see, some fetch a fiver, some are even free to a good home', she stormed. Plummer ignored her and showed an algebraic formula he had worked out on his hand. It was not a surprising drawing board as I'd seen him work out elaborate calculus problems, which had baffled university maths tutors, on the dust of lorries parked in cafe car parks and often wondered how the lorry cleaners must have felt when they saw these formulas on the back of trunkers. He ignored Sally and with irritating accuracy he said, 'I think you will need about 30 greyhounds to breed a number of puppies which will provide a liveable income, calculating X number of live puppies per litter, a constant stock of correctly bred greyhounds and a price that is well above the price charged for the average lurcher'.

'He's quite mad,' Sally erupted, 'what if they don't sell – and they won't at the price you are asking'. Plummer, unperturbed by Sally's attack on his sanity which he has undoubtedly heard before anyway, did yet another calculation on the palm of his hand. 'For about 20 months things will be a bit tough, but with the correct broods, properly reared whelps and only selected breeding from greyhound dams you are almost certain to succeed'. He referred to Sally's points concerning her reference to the number of puppies offered at next-to-no-price sums. 'They are mongrels, lanky hybrids not your type and quality,' he replied and added, 'Ford vans,' he kicked his own disparagingly, 'are always advertised and cheaply. Rolls Royces are never advertised and are never cheap.' 'A present', he said, offering Sally a dark brindle bitch sired by a Derby winner, and got back into the van. 'He's quite mad', Sally repeated yet again and Plummer who had done yet another calculation on the condensation of his window said, 'In 23 months you'll have made quite a name for yourself with lurchers', and drove off.

Actually the gift of three greyhound bitches in or near season was not such a terrible imposition. We were still killing off our broiler fowl and battery birds and had offal and heads enough to feed a dozen, though how Plummer had calculated 30 still puzzles me despite the fact that his figures have proved more or less correct. In school we toiled over Dodson's *Primary Maths* (by the writer whose pen name was Lewis Carroll, author of *Alice in Wonderland*) and laboured over crazy sums about how long it would take a bath to fill if both taps ran to the full and the plug was left out. Everyone hated these insane sums but I've often thought Plummer must have loved them, and life must have taken on a new meaning for him when he began to calculate sums from that most baffling genetic programme, Mendel's Law of Independent Segregation. He finds cars and machinery quite baffling and doesn't even try to understand when I explain the most rudimentary parts of a car's mechanism to him, but a baffling genetic problem is enough to entertain him for four days and nights and friend as he is he must be impossible to live with.

Sally, however, took to the brindle bitch immediately, house training it in minutes, breaking it to cats in days – no mean feat for the owner of a track greyhound, and a week later went to Plummer's curious cottage to mate her to his merle stud dog; Plummer predicting absolutely accurately the colours of the whelps which would result from the litter.

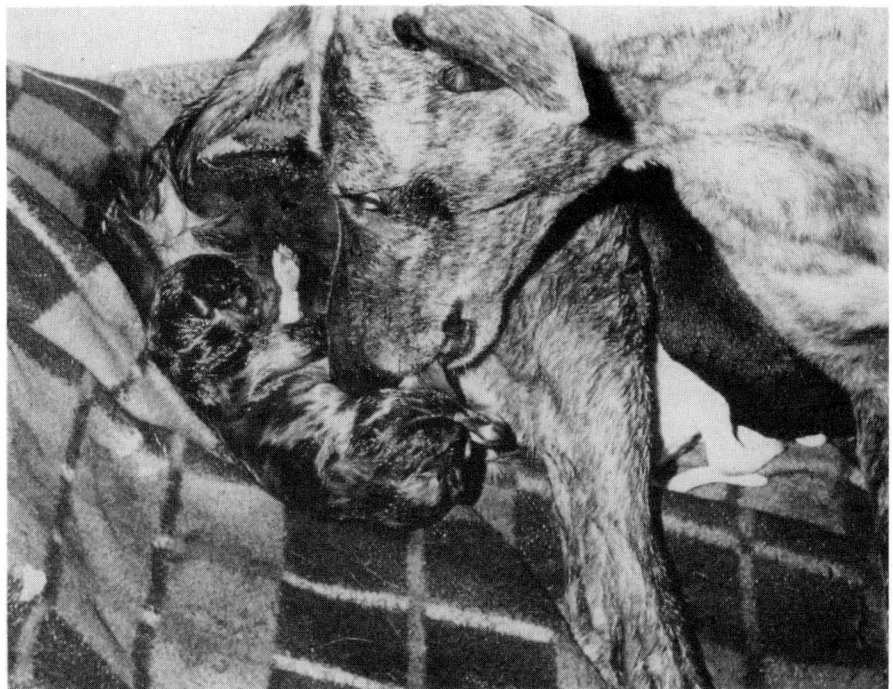

Simone giving birth to Romulus.

Simone, as Sally called the bitch, whelped in her bedroom in a box near
Sally's bed and before the first puppy, a sooty merle, had been licked
clean Sally had christened it Romulus and decided to keep it. We sold
the litter with a shade more difficulty than we expected and the sale of
the last puppy left a rather bitter taste in my mouth. We sell eggs at so
much a dozen, chickens at such and such a pound, and turkeys weighing certain weights are ordered and sold long before they are delivered
at Christmas. This sort of thing discourages hagglers of the type found
in Middle Eastern markets and frankly I dismiss hagglers, bidders or
idiots who want to swap dogs with a few terse, polite but sometimes
unrepeatable comments. We were left with one puppy from Simone, a
gay merle pied, the markings of which Merle produced in every litter he
bred. Funnily enough, and I am aware that colour is not related to
performance, the £3280 dog sold at Appleby was of this type and all the
gay pieds bred from Merle seemed to be outstanding. However, be that
as it may, pieds are sometimes the very devil to sell and striking looking
white dogs are overlooked when buyers step over them to examine
and buy indifferent brindles. It's a ridiculous prejudice but I am a

commercial breeder and the customer is always right – well almost always right even when he is patently wrong.

I was out for the day engaged with some business – buying seed or getting a van or something else – which made me leave the farm and I left my daughter Sally in charge. A fellow from Birmingham bowled up and asked to see the puppies and as I've mentioned we had only Timmy, our big gangling pied dog left. He was nine weeks old, unsocialised, and his odd brindle/merle markings made him perhaps a little less attractive than the rest of the litter which had just been sold. The buyer – actually another word just came to mind but I can't use it – examined the puppy, critically remarked that pieds weren't any good as they were conspicuous on dark nights and made a few disparaging comments before offering Sally £10 less than the price she'd asked. Sally had been put down by the chap a little and made aware of her own

Timmy at approximately 18 weeks.

ignorance of lurchers as this was the first litter she had bred. He gave all the patter of the real down-bidding conman and to cut a long story short, Sally sold him the puppy for the price he offered. Joan, my wife; listened to the tale and as unlikely as it sounds she has the gift of second sight (she predicted Plummer's heart attack). She said 'He'll be back'. Joan proved correct. Timmy was returned several weeks later and I quote, 'He's too timid and afraid of the older dogs'. Timmy was 12 weeks old at the time and had seen few people and even fewer dogs. We had another litter at the time bred from the pale fawn bitch and our dealer suggested a swop, Timmy for another puppy. Joan dealt with him quietly and efficiently, probably cutting him like a knife and simply returned his money telling him we had no more dogs to ruin and we weren't in the part exchange business and the messer shrank away.

Timmy was in excellent condition and I have to give the man that at least, but a puppy suffers mentally from chopping and changing and Joan who rarely puts her foot down or interferes with our breeding programme said quite simply, 'He stays now'. Sally promptly sold him

Romulus who still allows himself to be dressed up.

to Thomas, my youngest son, for the return price (yes, I'm afraid my kids are like that), and Timmy stayed.

Socialising, particularly in a collie lurcher, is vital and the difference between Romulus who slept, and still does, on Sally's bed and Timmy, who lived out, became monumental as time went on. Romulus learned tricks, played stupid games, allowed himself to be dressed up and generally became the family clown. Sally swore he hadn't a hunting instinct in his body and when he retrieved chickens to hand with the gentle soft mouth of a golden retriever, she believed this reinforced her view of Romulus' lack of hunting instinct. However, a chance incident proved Sally wrong – and how wrong the reader can realise by reading the next few lines.

As poultry farmers we are plagued with foxes. We've killed six in a night and still found poultry missing the next morning. One night I shut a fox in a poultry pen by mistake and he demolished the entire brood, escaping when I opened the hatch in the morning. We snare foxes if we can and Joan sells the pelts and gives the skinned bodies to Chinese clients who enjoy fox meat – it takes all sorts I suppose. Well,

Romulus crunching a fox long after it is dead.

one morning Romulus (who was often seen off by our ginger cat) chanced on a snared fox and wagging his tail sniffed it, it retaliated by nipping his nose drawing blood and he yelped and shot back. Seconds later he was shaking the now dead fox crunching every bone in its body with an almost insane fury and continued to shake the corpse long after the body had cooled. In seconds he had changed from a house dog that Sally was wont to dress up in ridiculous clothes, to a raging fiend, mad for any fox he encountered. He killed two foxes before he was 12 months old and has had an implacable hatred of them ever since. Sally, however, continued to dress him up in ridiculous clothes and he still kept clear of our ginger cat.

Timmy, who had not been socialised as much, was as different as chalk to cheese, he fought shy of picking up rabbits until the penny dropped and then he became the super athlete, faster than Romulus or Celt, able to come off hedges at an incredible pace, rabbit in jaws, but hide intact and bones unbroken. True he learned the hard way and met with awesome collisions receiving terrible bruising and concussion in his first few runs but from then on he developed an uncanny knack of turning on himself as he picked up off hedges and was seldom injured. He had and still does have an incredible nose and twice has run a hare so far by scent that he's no stranger to our local dog's home. We no longer let him wander alone, the cost of retrieving him is becoming prohibitive and dogs' homes are a bit disease prone. He ran on Salisbury Plain two summers ago alongside several longdogs (longdogs are crosses twixt sight hounds – greyhound/saluki, greyhound/whippet, greyhound/deerhound) and came away with the proud title of the fastest lurcher the longdog men had seen. I do so hope the meddler who returned him to us reads this tale – it's poetic justice I suppose. We lamped not only Timmy and Romulus but also Simone, their greyhound dam, who picked up the knack quite quickly for a greyhound, and as she is a shade faster than her sons, she puts up a good show at a hare until of course her greyhound stamina begins to ebb. Timmy's stamina is endless and I've run him alongside longdogs which have had to be carried back to vans while Timmy continued to romp away the night. We've retired him now or nearly so as his feet are beginning to play up and he's a little more injury prone after a hard night. Still, on good days he takes some beating, though after a bad collision his kidneys received a bit of damage.

Two years after the birth of our first puppies we began to get a name for breeding good class collie bred lurchers – almost exactly the way Plummer had predicted and started sending stock abroad. In all fairness, however, although we used Merle to the exclusion of all other dogs and his track record of producing top class workers is outstanding – he bred coursing champions, top-rate lampers like Steve Jones' noted bitch, all rounders like Timmy, Romulus, Celt and a score of others – he was not the perfect stud dog some of the *Shooting News* letters rate him to be. He had defects which he certainly passed on to his children and his puppies weren't everyone's cup of tea. They were irritatingly sensitive, refusing to work if chided, let alone smacked, quite slow to start, and his bitches by and large were undersized. When he turned off a top class male its performance made its owner a legend, but the number of good bitches he sired I could count on one hand and have a finger or so to spare. Plummer had predicted foot trouble in his progeny particularly in the lightly boned progeny and true to form many of his bitches went lame in later years. It became time to start to breed another stud dog and once more the prospects of producing such a dog were mused over for a long while before the dog was produced. I'll leave the subject of the Merle family with one point and I'm afraid I must disagree with Plummer over some of his theories no matter how accurately he has been able to predict the outcome of matings,

Plummer, in his book *Practical Lurcher Breeding*, states that the three quartered is the end of a line and should not be continued. I've used Romulus and Eddie Jones has used Celt on various bitches and both have bred a lot of useful lurchers, some of which have swept the board at meets and shows. Plummer argues that both have thrown up far too many greyhounds when mated to mongrel bitches, but sufficient to say I get repeat matings to Romulus time and time again, and as I've said the customer is always right — well nearly always.

One of Romulus's sons out of Graham Butler's collie cross bitch.

—5—

A New Stud Dog, New Line and a New Measure of Success

PLUMMER ESTIMATES IT took him 12 years to breed Richard Jones, and I know this to be correct, and only when Richard contracted a bronchial virus did I realise his value to my establishment and appreciate the long-proffered advice that I must breed a replacement for him. He has feet like soup plates, indestructible toes, metacarpels and metatarsals which just don't sustain injury and a coat which would resist an arctic wind going full blast. He ran wild for nearly two years, was hellish to break to the lead and has a hunting instinct which prevents him from being let off the lead or else he'd be gone. In short, he has the constitution of the toughest Scottish bearded collie (I'll dwell on this subject later), resembles the Polish Nizinny and has the quiet nature of the border collie clan. He is a born clown, an excitable dog to mate and has bred a few second-rate puppies I must admit, but a hell of a lot of first-rate stock as well. He will be sorely missed when he dies and at the time of writing both Plummer and I are going hell for leather to breed a replacement for him with roughly the same genetic make-up as the old chap himself.

He was a nuisance as a puppy and an uncontrollable nuisance at that. He ranged far and wide from Plummer's cottage, herded just about everything into tight little groups – people, dogs, sheep and above all the Huddlesford herd of champion Friesians, and when I was loaned him on a sort of permanent loan basis, Plummer breathed a sigh of relief, even though I had to curtail his freedom to prevent further nuisance in Sutton Coldfield.

To all intents and purposes he is a merle though he has such a profuse coat as to resemble an old-fashioned Welsh Grey, but genetically his make-up is far too complicated to be classed as simply a merle for he has been mated to certain greyhound bitches and produced harlequin-coloured puppies which not only baffled Plummer, who has written

47

Richard Jones with Phil Lloyd.

numerous scientific papers on merles and merle inheritance, but also stumped some of the world's leading scientists who correspond with him. Frankly his genetic make-up doesn't worry me two hoots. His stock has gone to some top-rate sportsmen, two of whom write for

Phil Lloyd with Maddie, his Richard Jones sired half cross.

Shooting News – The Warrener and Phil Lloyd, and they have done well with them. So whatever his colour make-up he has proved worth his weight in gold and he became the start of a new line, which after careful consideration, I believe to be superior to the line bred from Plummer's merle – my opinion – no, I believe I can back up my statement with solid, down to earth fact.

My leading stud dogs are bred from Richard and of course the dam of these studs was inevitably the Bauhus bitch, Sally, dam of Eddie Jones' Celt, Julie Love's cream merle, Hooten's Blue and a host of superb hunting dogs. Mated to a donkey Sally would produce a serviceable lurcher – though I admit I haven't tried the cross, but her progeny taken one stage further and mated to progeny from Linden Eland have served people well all over the world.

Eland, who was whelped in April 1970, took The Waterloo Cup field by storm in 1972, winning an exciting final against Hedera. Both finalists were Hi There bred, Eland through Hi There Merry, Hedera through Printer's Prince and of course Newdown Heather. Eland was not only a superb tactician on the field but could catch and kill like a lurcher and was such a prolific stud dog that most modern coursing greyhounds are related to him and there has been a tendency to inbreed to this dog. Possibly because Bauhus was not related to him, the progeny of Sally has clicked with that of Eland, and certainly my best three quarter bred puppies have come from Eland bred stock, or from tightly related Newdown Heather bred bitches. Lurcher breeding is partly a science and once the rules and laws have been proven only a fool doesn't stick with them.

Richard, the half bred beardie/border, bred to give border trainability and beardie skin, coat and tough feet, was a problem dog. To start with he had been left to run totally wild as a puppy, living as he pleased, sleeping where he wanted and wandering where he wanted. He had had total liberty and had developed sexual fetishes about sacks, a rather bewildered neutered collie from the end of the village, and a hideous plastic gnome some four feet high and rather garish coloured in a garden a mile or so away. It was not the best training for a stud dog and is in fact a bit damaging to the legitimate work a stud is to perform. To mate a bitch, even a very easy, well-tried matron like Sally with a dog of this background is difficult, and particularly as Richard is 21″ tall and Sally nearly 26″. After building a ramp of stone slabs and allowing Richard several exhausting attempts at a mating we decided to give it a miss and return the next day, leaving Sally woefully frustrated and Richard so exhausted as to refuse his food and forsake his daily visit to see the plastic gnome. Fortunately on the second day we managed to mate him after another exhausting effort, exhausting to Plummer, my wife Joan and Richard who tied with Sally and fell asleep during the mating. It was an absurd sight and one I could not resist photographing. He tied with Sally a further time before she began snapping at him indicating that she was no longer ready for service. She whelped her litter nine weeks to the day – a mix of merle and black collie-marked puppies and we phoned Plummer a day after they were born. He arrived with ruler and calipers, measured their backs, looked up and said quietly, 'They aren't what I'd want Dave,' but added, 'maybe it's due to the fact they've been allowed to suckle though'. It's a curious fact that puppies, particularly half bred, manifest their true

Taffy retrieving a rabbit on one of his first lamping outings.

shapes shortly after birth and even before they have a chance to dry. A clumpy puppy (cobby, short, leggy, heavy-boned; funnily, these usually make phenomenally good lampers), will appear very short-backed just after it is born while an elegant long-back dog (and despite popular opinion elegant half bred puppies are often produced) looks very long-backed at birth. Allow a litter to suckle and it is a different matter, within hours they will, providing they are born healthy and are not premature, look plump and of the same shape. A half bred should always be chosen at birth or after 12 weeks if one wants a looker that is, for some of the most useful puppies I've bred have been not the type to win at shows.

Two puppies stood out in the litter – a collie-masked, rough-coated dog which went to Nick Rollaston of Colchester and a pale blue merle, wall-eyed through and through, not just tick-eyed as the majority of white-eyed merles I've bred are. He grew up a hairy puppy and with those blue eyes staring out of the blue merle fur, my daughter Sally called him Yeti after the abominable snowman. Later I decided on a more reasonable name as he was bred as a stud dog to replace the now ageing Merle and plumped for Taffy.

Taffy was not an attractive puppy. At four months of age he kangarooed badly, throwing his hindquarters far too high as is often the case of many lurchers with bearded collie blood in them, but at six months he began to pull himself to some shape, growing into his hindquarters and losing his sway back. We lamped him as soon as he was well grown and although thick of limb and not yet putting things together he caught his first and returned it to hand. He was worked lightly after this for he was bred as a stud and had only to prove himself to justify his breeding, while Timmy and Romulus were in their prime and were receiving a lot, perhaps a little too much work as both Thomas and Sally had become fanatical lampers and were lamping not just the three quarter breds, but every greyhound bitch which would show an interest in following the beam. Again contrary to opinion

Monty's greyhound mother Black Bess retrieving a live rabbit.

many greyhound bitches particularly those with the inclination to carry things around in their mouths can make excellent lampers. We've had at least two which took readily to the lamp and while they lack the stamina of a properly bred lurcher, some will put many lurchers to shame at picking up rabbits or hares, though few show a great interest in sitters until the rabbit or hare shows the slightest movement of its ears or prepares to run.

Richard sired, after numerous crazy attempts, several litters in the next year or so and funnily enough there was an incredible enthusiasm for half bred puppies at that time, possibly because of lamping

52

enthusiasts. Generally speaking, three quarter bred puppies make the best sellers. They look the part, greyhoundy even at eight weeks of age and perhaps three out of every four puppies I sell are three quarter breds, though frankly should I be restricted to the ownership of one dog with time to train and ample place to enter I should plump for a good half bred any day of the week. Most are tougher-skinned, have better feet, resist wear, tear and knocks which go hand in hand with lamping and while it might be argued they have seldom the speed to come to terms with a hare except on the lamp it can also be argued that a great many pure bred sight hounds and three quarter breds don't do all that well either. Thomas, my son, owns a black dog called Monty, a Richard son out of a black track greyhound bitch which is just about what I'd want if I had only one dog. He's a good lamper, a fine jumper, biddable and doesn't think twice before tackling a fox. He has a fine, slinky shape, fast enough to be useful with legs which take knocks and feet which are just about uninjurable. We worked him on a broken-up aerodrome in the Isle of Man in 1984 and although he was pushed hard day and night – a little excessively I think as the group of hunters had a fair proportion of youths among them, and youngsters are apt to over-run lurchers. Monty's feet stood up to a terrific bashing and he came off the ferry on four feet without a toe out of place or a wrist slightly swollen. Some of the dogs we took had to be carried back each night so overworked were they, but Monty as the saying goes 'ran the spectrum'. Funnily enough he's smooth-coated and black and has only smooth-coated black puppies when put to greyhounds. Speed wise I

Monty about to strike his rabbit.

suppose he isn't quite up to a dog with a dash more greyhound added to a half bred mix but I rate him highly.

Funnily enough, after the first batch of Richard/greyhound puppies I had by first complaint about the stock I was breeding. A young man from Manchester had great trouble lead-training his puppy and almost gave up with her. Richard was a devil to lead-train and perhaps this strain of bearded collie used in his creation may be a little lead-shy, but I've had few other complaints about this problem and the puppies I've kept from Richard have all trained easily to the lead. Plummer, who regularly goes to Scotland to research bearded collies which are still at work there, has interviewed the breeders and some have lead-shy collies while others have not. Sufficient to say Maddie, the half bred Richard puppy supplied to Phil Lloyd, the *Shooting News* writer, was no problem on the lead and neither was the puppy purchased by Pat who writes under the name The Warrener for *Shooting News*. At one time I thought it was the fault of the dogs that I threw up the occasional rogue, the odd maverick which will not tolerate a lead, but I am now convinced that it is the fault of the trainer, as no competent, experienced

Eddie Jones' Celt, a great jumper.

lurcher trainer has ever complained about the lead training problems in puppies they have bought from Richard's getting.

Pros and cons, however, are the order of the day with every strain of lurcher and while several of Richard's stock are winning well in obedience tests only a few are lightly enough built to win in the show ring. It's not sour grapes but I don't rate the show ring as a place to set one's values regarding lurchers, though I must admit that I enjoy watching a man judge a show. It's a point of interest but Eddie Jones' Celt, a great work dog by any standards – a terrific jumper, hunter, a good lamper and a dog capable of working all day and all night – has been entered in many shows yet has barely been called out or placed in a show as judges consider him too heavy. Speed and certainly working ability has nothing to do with slender whippety shape and I've worked with a few show winners which have had to be carried back to the van long before heavy, bulkier dogs are even beginning to tire. I'm not blowing my own trumpet or trying to sell half bred stock, but a working lurcher shouldn't be indistinguishable from a greyhound, and should have an air of bulk and a lot of meat about him, particularly if he's a lamping dog and is required to run every moonless night and pick up 20, 30 or more rabbits a night. A whippety dog, light on bone and easy on the eye perhaps, may put up a splendid show on the first five runs or so but after that its resources seem to get a bit drained and it's at this time a heavier dog comes into its own. One point to make about any muscular lurcher or heavily built lamp dog: a whippety dog is easy to condition to get just right. Simply put him out of his shed once a week and he'll respond to the night's work as if he is run nightly. A heavily built lurcher, particularly a dog with a great deal of collie in its make-up needs to be run at exactly the right weight. Run too fine and he'll burn like a torch for the early part of the evening, run too heavy and he'll just not be up to picking up difficult rabbits. A hawk master knows exactly the right weight at which to fly his hawk, and while I don't advocate a lurcher man weighing his dog before each night's lamping there's a lot to be said for knowing the optimum weight at which a dog will perform best. Boxers, like Henry Cooper in his autobiography, state that they perform best when they are exactly a certain weight and lurcher lampers should get to know their dogs as well as an athlete gets to know his own body to get the best out of them.

While on the subject of half breeds there's an excellent story of Taffy's sister that is well worth relating at this point and well worth remembering I might add. Nick Flint, a clothing shop manager from Tamworth, bought two lurcher puppies from me at the time of Taffy's birth: a black sired by Merle out of a greyhound, and a full sister of Taffy, a replica apart from the fact half her face was white and the rest

Nick Flint's Peregrine.

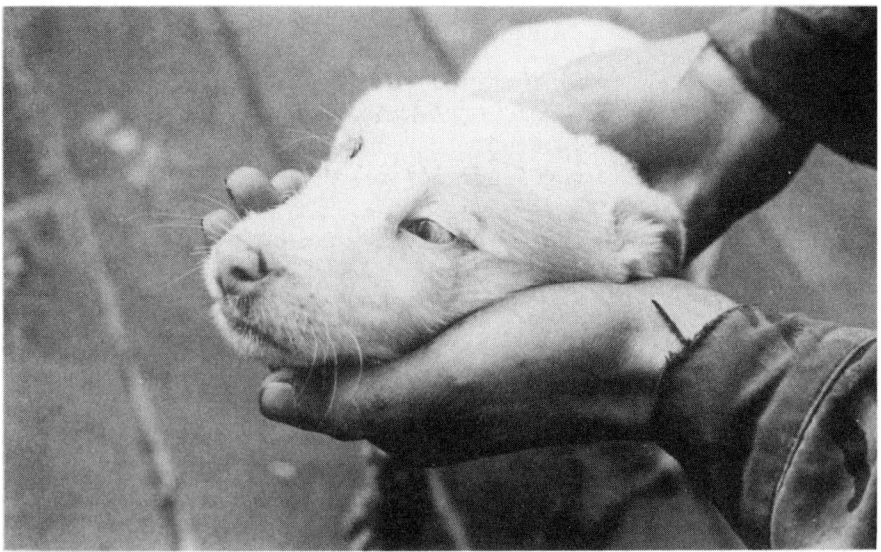

The blind and deaf pup in Nick Flint's litter.

was merle whereas Taffy is full merle-faced. Nick had the black destroyed after a hideous fall had driven leg bones through organs where leg bones should never be, but an odd quirk of fate caused Nick to breed a peculiar litter from the bitch. Plummer was having a lot of trouble with thieves and one day Flint who worked in Lichfield found a man with a blue bird tattooed on his neck leading Merle back to his van. He saw Nick and ran off leaving the dog to run loose and Flint offered to take the now ageing stud to his kennels to mind until the heat was off so to speak. The upshot of the matter was Merle served Flint's bitch (Richard to Sally). Merle to merle matings produce devilish monstrosities – Plummer has worked out why a dozen times or more for people on the dust of cars, vans or walls used as blackboards, but it does not make the slightest difference, every year some idiot believes he's right and tries to repeat the error. Flint's mating occurred by accident and I photographed the litter to add to my collection. One puppy was blind and deaf, another was partially sighted, but the rest were fine, and I believe Flint kept a black puppy which wins fairly regularly in shows – a little too heavy in the neck perhaps but anatomically an eye-catcher particularly in the collie classes which are becoming fairly popular at shows.

Taffy's sister, Linnet, is a good ferreting dog.

57

The litter sister of Taffy, a bitch called Linnet, possibly the best rough-coated half bred I have kept if not bred, cut a tendon and became a non-starter coursing wise – a pity as she was faster than Taffy and a better turner. She works ferrets well but then so do almost all of my other dogs which are fit, well and capable, so I suppose I keep her out of pure sentiment. I have a rule about lurcher breeding learned the hard way, and that is once one has developed a strict formula for breeding and the formula is working don't buck or vary the system. Hence I never breed from any bitch other than a greyhound, and never (well, I'll come to that later) breed lurcher to lurcher. Once and only once have I made an error and that was when Timmy just managed to mate Linnet. I've had excellent reports on the litter which according to simple maths are five-eighths bred greyhound/collies (Plummer assures me they are not and are simply 'variables') and I have had a few requests to breed another litter. Frankly I have refused, as a name as a 'messer' – a breeder of odds and sods, and God only knows there are enough in the Midlands – is not what I want, and on the subject of mistakes, or maybe miscalculations would be a better word, I'd better come clean about another abortive experiment which did me no good whatsoever and is one I'll not repeat.

I'd started getting a good name for breeding collie lurchers and all was going well and my place was the place to buy the real thing. I bred only collie crosses, never mixed breeds, never bred other crosses and was happy with the fact that I no longer got the 'do you breed saluki/deerhound or such and such' phone calls. I grew a little confident of my ability at this point and broke the cardinal rule and bred another cross. Max, our Alsatian or German shepherd guard dog, is a big vicious brute with strangers and if proof is needed we get no thefts. He killed Joan's two goats, which had just eaten half my garden, and this endeared him to me if not to Joan. I mated Max to a greyhound after a conversation with Geoff Battans who appears in Lambourn and who killed maybe 210 deer with a cross which could have been (and I'm a bit guarded about this statement after seeing photographs of Battans' dogs) an Alsatian/greyhound hybrid and was assured by the Bedfordshire contingent the produce would sell like hot cakes (Plummer winced and said nothing else about the subject). Eddie Jones came daily to see the puppies and I was quite pleased with the results. They didn't sell – I gave quite a few away though I am sure they would have been excellent hunters, but worse still a story got round I was breeding this cross and turning away from collie/greyhounds. It was a disastrous error of judgement and one I was glad to live down. Battans had one – I gave it to him, but the rest we had to dispose of. Perhaps they make excellent hunters – certainly some people swear by them as German

Max.

German shepherd × greyhound lurcher owned by John Hancock.

shepherd dogs often make really top class hunters and a dash of greyhound gives better conformation, more speed and a shade more thrust. Still it's an experiment I shan't repeat in a hurry. This book is meant to be an accurate chronicle of my time with lurchers and people who don't make mistakes write only for sporting magazines. I made my mistake breeding this hybrid. Enough said, now back to the Richard line.

Taffy on the alert.

Taffy became sexually mature at this time and being free from his sire's fetishes he became a damn good stud. Richard is after every bitch he sees in or out of season and even gets just a bit friendly with other males. Taffy knew instinctively when a bitch was ready to stand and neither took an interest nor went into courtship display until the bitch considered herself ready. He mated easily, tying without fuss and never once making a fool of himself, as Richard still does just about every time he serves a bitch. I must stop making fun of Richard. He was ill the other day and only then did I realise how priceless he was, how great a loss he would be and how I must at all costs breed an identical genetic replacement for him. Taffy too was to become an irreplaceable stud, but his progeny had to be tested and until it was I still used the aged, fat, and now grumpy Merle to breed my three quarter breds. Never a reliable or eager stud he was now becoming very lack-lustre in his attitude to mating and made half-hearted attempts to mate even the most oversexed bitches. Taffy arrived just at the right time, though we produced one or two more litters of Merle's puppies before we used Taffy almost exclusively to breed three quarter breds.

Taffy was an instant success as a stud. Most three quarter breds, if one of the parents is a border collie/greyhound first cross, are smooth-coated and while they do the job well enough – that's an understate-ment, most are outstanding – they are never really glamorous and the smooth coat makes them almost indistinguishable from greyhounds. Some of Taffy's first litter were silky-coated and beautiful even as puppies and conformation wise were hard to fault. Some resembled deerhound hybrids and a few were really dazzling looking merles, merles of every colour, shade and hue and there are supposed to be 64 variations of merle colouration and possible marking. I've bred cream merles, red merles, harlequins, dun merles, which I find beautiful though they are not to everyone's taste not by a long chalk, and some really spectacular pied merles.

Pieds, or rather the public's attitude to pied lurchers, has undergone a change since I bred poor old Timmy who is now just that – poor old Timmy! People now actually choose a white puppy out of a coloured litter and while many old hands won't touch a gay pied (more white than colour) there are those who would like to see a white lurcher class run at shows. Frankly, I'm neither for nor against the colour. I'm a professional lurcher breeder admittedly specialising in the one strain, but my task is simply to satisfy clients whatever their whims and colour preferences. I avoid 'pushing' a pied if people are a little anti that colour, but then perhaps I've learned something from my experience with Timmy. Anyway, to bring an end to this mass of comments concerning pied lurchers, anyone who uses a merle lurcher or collie to breed lurchers will throw up a fair number of pieds regardless of the collie or the colour of the greyhound used, so the breeder of merle-coloured lurchers must get used to more than his share of white 'uns. Plummer's Merle threw them, and Taffy has turned off some raging beauties, but as I've said they're not everyone's choice. Anyway, it's time to move on to another aspect of the book before the reader reckons I've a fixation about a particular family of lurchers and refuse to talk about anything other than that family.

—6—

A Few Collies Too Many

RICHARD, THE HALF bred bearded border collie, was the first collie to be used in our breeding project, but he was by no means our only line of collie to produce lurchers. Our second collie was a rather curious gift, at least I think it was a gift. We had invited Plummer over for Christmas dinner as we do each and every year and he had decided to come. He'd sat throughout our festivities, eaten his food, watched a Roman film, made a few comments that the producer was wrong about the dates and the battle plan of a particular army, and out of the blue said to Joan, 'I'll buy you a pure bred bearded collie as a Christmas present'. Neither Joan nor I had ever thought of owning such a dog and besides that Brian was flat broke at the time. 'When will you get it?' said Joan. 'Don't know really', Plummer remarked and added, 'Spartacus' name was probably Zapardocus, but the Romans mutilated Greek names,' and dropped the subject. He left in this tiny Fiat 126 saying, 'Buy one and I'll pay for it'.

A word perhaps on the nature of bearded collies and the people who breed them. When Mrs Willison resurrected the bearded collie in 1948 there was still quite a few working strains about regardless of what the book may imply. She simply took the most elegant, mated it to the most elegant, and produced the long flowing coats of her first Crufts winners. Perhaps some breeders added a dash of old English sheepdog – delightful, silly and absolutely brainless balls of fur – to improve coat, though most breeders deny it, and we'll leave the matter at that. Sufficient to say that the working bearded collie is a million miles away from the show beardie in shape, coat, constitution but more important still in brains and stamina.

Working beardies are getting less numerous each year and more's the pity. Borders are now in vogue and if the British public aren't too careful they may find the bearded collie, the worker not the show dog, kept simply by a few people of the sort who still breed Gloucester Old Spot pigs just to keep the breed alive. Having said that there are those who very fairly level criticism at the good old-fashioned bearded collie. They start herding late in life sometimes as late as three years old, though the trial bug has produced strains of dog which herd literally from the nest. Beardies also have a reputation for 'balling' and that's nothing rude, it simply means their coats become matted with mud in summer (when the majority are incidentally sheared like sheep), or worse still with snow at a time of year when they need every scrap of coat they can carry, particularly in Perthshire or anywhere between Perth and Tongue for that matter where the climate is bad for nine months and hellish for the remaining three.

Remus, my Scottish beardie, snow balled.

So much for the cons, but there are a hell of a lot of pros as well. Nothing short of an Eskimo dog is tougher than a beardie, some prefer to be out in the snow, sleet and all stations below zero. They will run all day and some will outwork any border on a hard day's gathering. Furthermore, in recent years there have been increasing numbers of complaints from Scottish shepherds of having difficulty in finding border collies which will 'face the hill' (work away from the shepherd or in several square miles of ground so rough as to be pasture fit for mountain goats). Some blame the trial craze for this defect and state that the trial-bred dogs are only circus performers, of little use in the field or rather 'on the hill' (a Scottish term used to describe any rough land not suitable to be used as arable). I've never heard this criticism levelled at the bearded collie, in fact many prefer to work far away. Most give tongue a bit – a quality which is essential in very hilly country to bring sheep in and keep them together – and this would be the kiss of death for their chances in a working sheepdog trial which demands absolute silence from a dog and disqualifies any dog which babbles in order to control the flock. Field trials although designed to resemble real life situations, are a far cry from the conditions found on the hill where sheep rest beneath sheltering crags and boulders aptly named 'roche moutones' (sheep rocks), and in these conditions the bearded collie comes into its own. They also tend to tag reluctant movers, nipping, putting in the odd bite or so, to speed them along and while this may also disqualify them at the trials, it's a priceless knack if the dog has to shift an old black-faced ram which doesn't give much of a damn for man or dog. I've seen beardies get rammed, battered, trampled and tossed by such rams, only to get up, take a breather to literally get the lungs working, and set to work with a vengeance to shift the ram.

There's a hell of a lot of debate as to whether the finely honed herding intelligence of the border collie is greater than the intelligence of its beardie counterpart and there are quite a few who believe that *One Man and His Dog* has set an irresistible trend which will ruin the initiative and replace intelligence with finely tuned herding instinct. While I can not claim to be an expert on collies, tales one hears from lurcher breeders who have used trial-bred collies on greyhounds to produce lurchers and have produced stark staring lunatics are by no means uncommon. Anyway, virtues and vices aside, Joan and I were left with the unenviable task of tracking down a suitable breeder from whom to buy Plummer's Christmas present for Joan, which must seem a ridiculously incongruous situation on the face of it, but as with all presents. 'it's the thought that counts' – or is it! We back-tracked half of Britain following up every lead until we came to a shepherd who worked the Pentland Hills around Dunsyre and who frequently bred a litter of bearded collies. Muirhead was approaching retirement but was as nimble and fleet as Steve Cram up and down those hills which left Joan and I breathless.

Tom Muirhead with his beardies.

Most working beardies, if not all in Scotland, are related in part to Muirhead's Dunsyre dogs – though most shepherds will be a little reluctant to admit the fact until questioned quite carefully. Moorhead of Dunbeath, who breeds a tall beautiful strain of bearded collie and who bred Paul Turnbull's, of Scots Gap, dog Blue (Britain's most famous bearded collie and the only one to be accepted at the National Sheepdog Register), which has a dash of Dunsyre blood in its veins as have the bearded collies of Steel of Denny, Stirlingshire, who keeps a strain of very hardy working blue and red beardies. Anyway, it was from Muirhead we bought the puppy, a blue-black beardie, typical of the drover's type dog used for the Galloway droves, and true to his word Plummer paid up. 'We're calling him Remus', we mentioned in passing, and Plummer glancing at Sally's huge merle lurcher Romulus which had recently pulversied a fox commented, 'In Plutarch's book Romulus killed Remus!' Not an easy man to live with, not by a damn sight I'm afraid!

Remus we kept shut up in a shed for nearly a month, not for the sake of any cruelty but because we had an outbreak of a disease which just could have been parvo virus on the farm and the beardie coming from uninoculated stock and being bred in a district where parvo is unknown would have been certain prey to the bug. We inoculated him and I feel his spell of imprisonment must have damaged him a shade as he was difficult to socialise at first, coming on call immediately but staying just out of catching distance. It took maybe a year to break that habit which

Remus under a tractor just out of catching distance.

Remus giving one of our guard dogs the collie eye.

I'm convinced was the result of my complete lack of socialising rather than nervous temperament. Nervous he just isn't and is reluctant to back down to any of our Alsatian guard dogs which patrol the place. Every adult lurcher is prey to his tormenting and more than once I gave heed to Plummer's quote from Plutarch's *Lives*, as he dices with death with some really powerful lurchers. IQ wise – well he's hard to beat, a bit wilful maybe and not all that keen on discipline, but he's as Teddy Moritz says, 'a cute sort of dog'.

Beardies have a reputation for a rare turn of speed equal if not exceeding that of the border collie. I've tested this one night when we lamped the Dyatt estate with Romulus, Timmy and Remus who rather ungraciously accepted the lead. He learned the meaning of the beam in seconds and had speed to spare in coming up with the rabbits. Slightly smaller than most of Muirhead's dogs, it would be interesting to see how a somewhat leggy bearded would perform on the lamp, particularly over rough country such as certain places in Perthshire. Speed they certainly have, stamina is without question, and the number of shepherds from Caithness to Morpeth who claim to have caught hares with beardies leaves one in no doubt that the hunting instinct is still intact.

Jake, the son of Remus, half beardie half greyhound, which I kept back for myself.

Remus was used at stud a bit later than we intended as he was small and looked like growing a bit more and I am reluctant to use an immature dog at stud. He stood stud to a brindle greyhound bitch and produced an extraordinary litter of deerhound-looking puppies, some of which made 26″ at the shoulder while the smallest bitch topped 23″. The coats of these puppies were ideally harsh, weatherproof and immune to the elements and I kept one back deliberately to watch him grow. As first crosses they take some beating as they are typey, good-looking and as keen as mustard. I've mated him since and produced an even better litter. All in all I couldn't be more pleased with our gift-horse Christmas present. Next year when his first sons and daughters are old enough to be classed as seasoned workers we'll know more of his potential – though judging from the interest shown in his puppies I think Remus may well make a more than just suitable stud particularly for the production of lampers where stamina and brains are more to be desired than just speed alone.

About four years before we acquired Remus, Plummer had begun writing to Dr Philpotts, a London eye specialist now retired and sadly unwell, who had some fascinating theories about the development of the modern working collie, its metabolism and almost obsessional interest in herding. He had written for the rare breeds magazine *The Ark* and had a *Star Trek* Dr Spock-like sense of logic which so appeals to Plummer, who believes no scientific fact unless it is proven twice over. Philpotts' theories on collies were interesting and as Plummer was making a TV show at the time I went to see him. I met the bed-bound Dr Philpotts in his house in Guildford and was immediately struck by his charm and careful thinking. Philpotts argues that another 20 years will see the end of the working life of the trial-bred collies, which are instinctive and also destructive herders, and which will herd flocks pointlessly and ceaselessly until both stock and dogs are nearly dead with exhaustion. Philpotts is also interested in the fact that he has evidence to show that the dietary needs of these habitual herders are greater than of the more primitive herding dogs, partly due to difference in structure but largely due to the nervous energy expended by dogs which are so hell-bent on herding. Funnily enough, Argue of Tain, a highly respected dog expert, had written to Plummer that same week stating that the prize of Britain's brightest dog did not belong to the trial-bred collies who lived on nervous energy and exaggerated instinct to do their 'Saturday five sheep in a fixed exercise', as my hill shepherds call the trials.

Philpotts had gone to Ireland for his initial stock which were quite similar to some of the more primitive breeds which probably gave rise to border collies and some of them had docked tails. The upshot of the interview was that I bought some of Philpotts' stock and now have a fair range of collie types from which to choose.

Gyp, Chuck Arrowsmith's border collie.

However, we added one more collie to our entourage or rather a half bred collie/greyhound if one wants to be exact. A gypsy family called the Arrowsmiths who live in Walsall had bought a blue merle collie from Appleby, Cumbria, during the fair and had mentioned to Joan and I that while he had had a lifetime of lurchers he had yet to encounter a better rabbit hunting dog. We toyed with using the dog for months before making our decision and finally mated a borrowed Hardly Ever sired greyhound bitch to the dog, keeping back a merle-coloured dog called Chuckles (Chuck Arrowsmith owned the dog hence the play on words). He has proven exceptional with a fine nose, great vigour and boundless energy and his first puppies are leaving me as I write. A three quarter bred from such a dog should be the very ticket, but only a fool predicts the outcome of such a mating.

69

Chuckles retrieving a rabbit.

—7—

Greyhounds in Number

OUR FIRST STOCK greyhound was my daughter's dog Simone, a track bitch bought at a sale by Steve Jones of Swadlincote and given as a present to Sally. Simone (no, I wouldn't have called her that), was a pet as much as a brood and though she had undergone remarkably little socialising as a puppy and had been a heller on cats, she settled in as a house pet, tolerating if not exactly liking our cats, and deliberately turning her head away when one of them approached her. I've always had the feeling that a greyhound is sold a bit short intelligence wise and Simone certainly proved it. She slept in Sally's bedroom, allowed herself to be dressed in ridiculous clothes, learned the type of tricks a collie learns and went like a thunderbolt in the field daytime or night. She put many lurchers I have seen to shame and her death left an unhappy period of several months in our family.

A greyhound bought as a whelp, reared in the house and properly socialised is a fairly unknown quantity regarding the question of IQ, and I once set out to breed my own strain of greyhound which could have been given the run of the farm like my lurchers, but that's another tale. At first Sally, the Bauhus bitch, was kennelled, but she lost so much condition and vigour at being restricted that she now enjoys total freedom. As a brood she has earned her corn a hundred times over. Her grandsons and granddaughters have gone all over the world and I've no complaints.

Greyhounds are not like other dogs or maybe not like other mammals in the way they come in season though their sexual cycle resembles that of a pig in reverse perhaps. Pigs come in season every three weeks, but allow a sow to miss a mating or so after she is mature and she is the very devil to get back in pig. Once started they are simply breeding machines or used as bacon. Greyhounds are the exact opposite in a manner of speaking, some are four or five before their bodies decide to come into season – though I am deeply suspicious of the use of oestrogens to bring a bitch into season quickly before a big race and it's

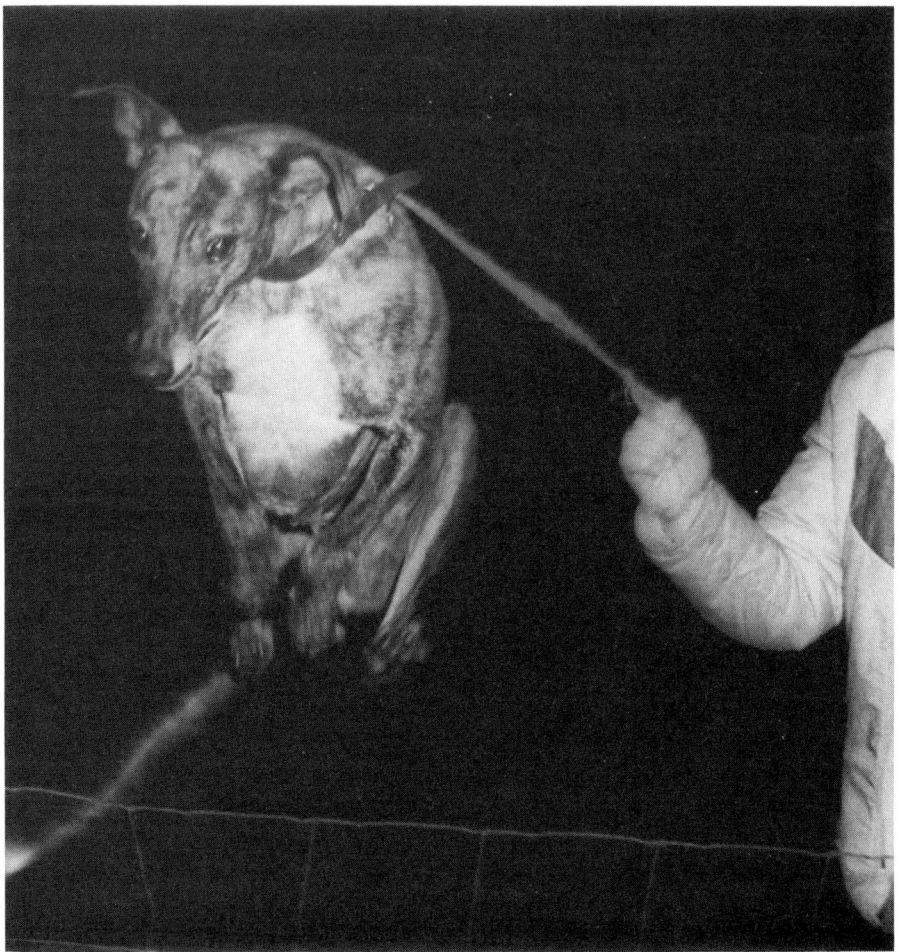

Simone jumping.

possible, just possible, that this treatment alters the breeding cycle of the bitch.

Another point of interest, indeed of interest to me as a breeder more than to the owners of track greyhounds perhaps, is the fact that most trackers during their racing years are 12-monthly bitches coming into season every year just once unlike the common or garden dogs which 'break down' every six months. However, kennel breeding greyhounds together and bred from them and in no time flat as soon as they produce their first litter they come in season every six or eight months and keep to that cycle. There are a number of reasons I can suggest for this peculiarity, the first being that once whelped every chemical used to continue artificial seasons while the bitch is racing is leeched out of the bitch's system and the bitch reverts to being an ordinary dog rather than just a running machine. She can now have a normal life uninhibited by chemical injections which determine when she is biologically ready to breed, or more to the point in the case of track greyhounds, not to breed. Another reason may be that bitches kept in number and allowed to mate and breed naturally must give off a scent which is slightly different from that of a track kennel where little breeding is attempted or accomplished, and it's a known fact that bitches in season kennelled with a reluctant breeder tend to induce the reluctant breeder into season. Perhaps this is an explanation though it would be the very devil to prove.

At first I suppose I took just about every healthy track reject and, track-damaged bitch; hoary veterans who had tired their hearts out and been put out to pasture – well, that's a bit of a fib, but I'm reluctant to mention the fate of most greyhounds. In all fairness most bred me some excellent puppies but in recent years I've become more choosy about which bitches best suit my dogs and I now turn down most of the bitches I am offered and deliberately shut off my mind to what I know will happen to most of them.

Some lines are much better than others for the production of lurchers and I must confess that I have a preference for Irish bred bitches. Plummer raved on about Bauhus when I met him first and still prefers bitches that carry lines to Bauhus' sire, Solar Prince. Bauhus went to the States in his prime so there are few of his progeny up for grabs. My own personal preference is I admit for the dogs bred from Linden Eland. Eland was a smallish, some consider slightly undersized dog owned by Mr A S Cathcart and trained by Hartley Dawes who had the knack of getting the Eland just right for every course. In addition to the inevitable Hi There line which had thrust and plenty of pluck, Eland's dam line carried Old Kentucky Minstrel, one of Dick Ryan's best wards. Minstrel had an uncanny knack of not only predicting the movements of a hare, but also a turning ability to compensate when a dog overshot the line of a hare. Thus breeding wise and temperament wise the descendants from Eland are first choice as far as I'm concerned and I've never so much as bred a suspect dog from his stock.

Temperament is all important, however, and I just don't want even the very best bred greyhounds if they have nervous temperaments or doubtful dispositions. A nervous dog is as much use as a sick headache,

they are a constant worry at feeding times as many are nearly impossible to catch if they escape. Furthermore, a nervy, jumpy dog is a dead
cert for causing kennel fights as others see its panic and strike at it – and
believe me greyhound fights have to be seen to be believed. The blood
and gore of the video nasty, *Texas Chainsaw Massacre*, wouldn't hold a

Bridie and Black Bess, two old greyhounds who are quite happy to live together.

candle to the sights which can be produced when a jumpy dog starts off
a full-scale kennel fight.

Greyhound bitches are best kennelled singly or at the most in pairs
and then feeding times are thwart with perils. To kennel three is
possible but there is always an element of risk about doing this as the
smallest incident can spark off a fight which would need a Larry
Holmes type kennelman to stop. For this reason I avoid accepting
known fighters even from the very best bloodlines – the damage such
animals will do outweighs their usefulness a hundred times over. Strong
bitches which react to insult quickly and firmly are not a problem, but the
trouble-seeker, the bitch willing to make a mountain out of a molehill in
kennels is not worth keeping. These aren't theories which have come out of
thin air, they are opinions based on experience at that.

The three greyhounds I was using to breed my own brood bitch. Left Hoover Junior, centre a Linden Eland sired bitch and right a Hardly Ever sired bitch.

At one time I entered into partnership to breed a level pack of inbred/linebred Eland whelps, but I dislike partnerships which are thwart with danger and certainly don't work out exactly as one plans them to. After a while I disassociated myself from the project and restocked with more adult Eland bred or preferably linebred bitches. I shan't attempt such a project again though perhaps the results may have justified the expense and effort of rearing a greyhound litter to simply breed lurchers. The fact is one of simple economics. I know some of the top class coursing greyhound breeders in the country, have ready access to their tried tested and over-the-top bitches and I breed only from the best available cast greyhound. Thus, it is not worth my while breeding my own greyhounds when I have ready access to the best over-the-top greyhounds.

Greyhounds are not the easiest bitches to mate – though my studs receive quite a lot of work and need little help in the mating process. A stud dog is worth so much that it is frankly madness to work him too hard and when trained to mate and handle even difficult bitches his value is increased tenfold, so to place a value on such studs is impossible. I usually muzzle a greyhound bitch about to be mated as it saves damage to the stud and also the person holding the bitch, and I've seen a bitch about to be penetrated bite out with awful fury at the person holding her.

Greyhounds however are amongst the easiest bitches to whelp. Caesarian sections, while not unknown by any means, are fortunately rare and usually occur in bitches which are either elderly and really past their breeding age or in bitches which have either an abdominal or uterine disorder – I had one of these, a black bitch which twice produced a litter of dead and partially mummified puppies which had to be extracted by Caesarian section. However, the majority of greyhounds which are well kept and well exercised are usually as easy as pie and certainly don't give the problems of some of the other breeds my wife has bred. Thousands of years of rigorous selection has produced a truly remarkable animal not overly bright perhaps, but a wonderful piece of construction nevertheless.

However, before the reader runs away with the idea lurcher breeding is simply a matter of beer and skittles, there are numerous snags concerning the keeping of greyhounds in number on a farm which not only houses dogs of other breeds – I breed Fell terriers and a variety of Jack Russells. Greyhounds straight off the track, less still from the coursing field, one must admit are seldom stockbroken and are keen to run and kill anything which is likely to give flight – a sheep, a goat, even a piglet, or anything smaller than they are. Terriers are particularly troublesome as they bark and irritate even calm bitches and stir up such a state of frenzy that sooner or later something has to 'give' – and it is usually the terrier's neck. Forget the silly old adage that a terrier will work under a big dog causing damage to rib, loin and a few other more private places. A terrier in a fracas with a greyhound is invariably a dead terrier long before the kennel man has a chance to part the combatants. I've lost several terriers in greyhound/terrier tussles which usually commence over the most trifling matters and I've spent hundreds of pounds in vet's fees getting shattered terriers repaired –

repaired but seldom serviceable I'm afraid, for the severity of a bite of a greyhound is seemingly out of proportion with the long, elegant jaws.

The other problem of keeping greyhounds is that they live a life of Riley at kennels, either track or coursing, and are hearty eaters from the time they arrive. Admittedly I've never found a 'picky' eater, one reluctant to wolf down food, quite the contrary in fact and greyhounds are usually very accommodating in what they eat. We feed a mish-mash of tripe biscuit and some complete dog food, usually boiling any flesh and drying off the meat stew with biscuit meal. A greyhound will devour a pile of this mixture and if I get away with £60 on dry bitches (bitches without puppies), I've had a very fortunate week indeed. Add to this the inevitable vet's bills, for greyhounds are injury prone, and as I refund money if a puppy dies and inoculation is a must, it's a hard job to stay afloat financially. Some weeks my bills make me feel quite sick and I wonder how in hell I'm going to soldier on. Something usually turns up and thankfully I have a market garden and a damn hard-working wife who is willing to work from dawn to dusk on market stalls selling our plants, sometimes in temperatures which are so cold that I feel ashamed she is out there. To succeed at any project a family must pull together – and thank God mine does.

Ear tattooing.

—8—

A Few of My Own Little Foibles Regarding Lurchers

A FEW STRAIGHT from the shoulder comments are necessary now, and straight from the shoulder they are. I love lurchers and greyhounds and travel miles to watch a coursing meet. However, I breed them to make a living and I can't be straighter than that if it's truth the reader is after. I breed honestly, I never lie about the breeding of a puppy – difficult as I breed only two crosses – never ever buy in puppies and sell them as my own (a common way of making a quick pound or so), and I endeavour to breed the best lurchers I can. I make a few mistakes, but I never repeat them, and my puppies are not only reared under heat lamps, but are also ear tattoed, so as to check on the performance of my stock. As I've mentioned I make no bones about the fact I am a professional lurcher breeder and to justify the word professional – a curiously misused word these days – I must have certain codes of ethics and stick to them rigidly. I make it a strict rule never to hard sell a puppy – pushing a 'not quite what I want' baby on to some client, as that's a sure way of making a few quick pounds and an even worse name! I never push a three quarter bred on to a man out to buy a half bred to course hares (though I do suggest the dog may not be fast enough), and I try my best never to sell two puppies to a person. Two lurchers are impossible to train and while an armful of lurchers paraded around the shows looks good, one or at the most two lurchers will do the job just as well. Please don't get me wrong, there have been times when finances were such that I would have loved to sell a whole litter to some chap or other as I've been somewhat more than short of cash. However, I'm in lurcher breeding for 'keeps' and a good name is hard to come by and easily lost – and the best way to get a good name is by reputation.

I usually refund money to customers who aren't satisfied with their puppies – and some of the reasons why puppies are returned are hilarious – 'He barked in the house'; 'He wet the floor'; 'I'm going away'; 'I'm going "inside", and it looks like I'm going down for a long spell this time'! I breed the best stock I can, I don't claim it to be the world's greatest – but the rest of the training and entering, the finishing touches, are or rather should be put in by the buyer and one point I

Wendell.

should make before passing on to a subject other than puppies, when I mark out a puppy to keep it is not for sale – no matter what the price, no matter what the financial state of my family. Sally, my daughter, has been offered a heck of a price for her three quarter bred rough-coated merle dog Paddy (Taffy × a coursing greyhound) but he is still with us inspite of the fact Sally could use the money. Several months ago I bred a replacement for Taffy – I call him Wendell and he's sired by Richard out of Taffy's mother. I have been inundated with requests to sell him as he's a damn sight more attractive than Taffy. To sell a dog one has deliberately bred as a stud is madness and a little like a carpenter selling his tools before taking up the job he is about to start. I sometimes run on maybe two studs and sell the one I don't particularly think justifies keeping, but never the other one.

On now to the subject of stud dogs and I know my idiosyncracies about these have caused more than just a bit of controversy in the sporting papers, so perhaps it is time to explain. Firstly, it behoves me to explain what I use as studs lest the reader should be confused by the names that follow.

Richard: A bearded/border collie stud very long-coated and a prodigious producer; he came from a litter of twelve and he has bred twelves.

Taffy: A blue merle; blue-eyed, rough-coated half cross rising 25" and a well-used stud by any standards.

Remus: A full bred working strain bearded collie, steel grey and 20" tall who has a propensity to produce tall first crosses.

Romulus and Timmy: Two merles. Timmy is a gay tan pied merle, Romulus is a sooty merle. Both are sired by Plummer's Merle and out of a greyhound bitch, Simone.

Jake: A pale red fawn half bred sired by Remus out of a good coursing bitch. He's 23" and resembles a deerhound cross.

Monty: A black, smooth-coated half bred sired by Richard out of a black greyhound; a good all-rounder, game as a pebble and fast for a half bred with super feet and boundless energy.

Chuckles: A half bred stud out of Chuck Arrowsmith's collie and a good sturdy coursing bitch. Chuckles is 23", has a super nose and is very keen. He's a sooty merle, not an attractive colour, but his first litter to a greyhound has produced some pale sky-blue merles with tight but dense coats.

So that's the toute ensemble and now for the rules regarding the use of these studs – and I won't budge an inch from these rules regardless of the price. Richard is not to stud to any bitches be they greyhound, sight hound or lurcher. He's a mainstay and a stranger with an eye to set up a rival lurcher kennel could use him, keep a puppy and be in competition with me instantly. He took Plummer 12 years to produce and I owe Brian that at least; so Richard – not at stud to any bitch.

Taffy is at stud at a higher price than any of the other studs but only, I must add, to any bitch other than a greyhound, no matter how unsuitable they may appear. He's a fairly level producer so no one is cheated. A greyhound or a bitch I suspect of being a greyhound – I always check ears – is not allowed near him. I produce an enormous

Richard Jones.

Taffy.

Remus.

Romulus.

Monty.

Chuckles.

Timmy.   *Jake.*

number of top class three quarter breds from him, to allow others to do so is cutting my own throat. Taffy throws a level crop to cur-bred lurchers. His three quarter breds mated to particularly good greyhounds are party-stoppers. No professional carpenter is prepared to lend his saw. Likewise I refuse to mate Taffy to greyhounds.

Monty, his half-brother, is at open stud and is covering greyhounds, sight hound crosses and lurchers. I'm not happy about his use on greyhounds as he's turning off some top-grade stuff, but he's my son's so I've little say in the matter though I'd as soon restrict his use to lurchers.

Timmy and Romulus are at open stud. Plummer in his *Practical Lurcher Breeding* is a bit shy of using three quarter breds because of the tendency to produce mainly straight greyhounds. Romulus has produced some good obedience winners mated to some lurchers. Curiously, Timmy possibly because he is a pied has had little chance at stud, though his speed puts others on my premises to shame.

Both Chuckles and Remus' son are at the moment at open stud and have as yet been only lightly used. Their stock is a bit of an unknown quantity and I may restrict the pair to lurcher matings.

As I've said I'm not in the business of upgrading other people's lurchers nor equipping competitors. My reasons for the choice of bitch accepted are strictly economic and neither money nor fair faces will make me change my mind. I sometimes get asked for dogs exclusively for hare coursing and while I admit that I've taken quite a few hares with my three quarter breds, I don't recommend them as strictly hare-catching dogs and suggest tactfully the enquirer had better buy a longdog, greyhound or a saluki which will do the job of hare coursing better than a lurcher. It's the truth and it pays to tell it no matter what the customer believes. I breed work dogs – dogs for lamping, dogs for all-round work, but I'm not a producer of dogs strictly for hare coursing.

I'm rarely asked for exotic crosses such as borzoi/Bedlington or saluki/Irish terriers and I certainly don't breed them. I learned my lesson about producing exotics the hard way with my Alsatian/greyhound litter. However, I do keep a notebook of folk who do breed exotics and pass on their names. These crosses are not my cup of tea, but then it wouldn't do for everyone to think the same way would it and what pleases me probably wouldn't please the man out to acquire an exotic.

Finally, Plummer an avid collector of tales of the near lunatic, always asks me to record phone calls of the sort which end, 'You know **** all about lurchers, Hancock', and for a while I did get a few of these, but now they are few and far between and I am seldom troubled when some poor, disturbed soul decides to spout off at 2 am and vent his spleen on someone.

Plummer becomes desperately upset when his phone rings at God forsaken hours, but I find most amusing, some a little sad and one or two rather annoying, but I am never upset by the chap who wishes to make war on the world.

—9—

Letter From America

TEDDY MORITZ IS really Theodora Moritz, an all American lady descended from German stock. Her interest in the chase is well known on both sides of the Atlantic and reports of her catches regularly appear in sporting magazines. Teddy hunts ground hog marmots or whatever they are called in particular states, and uses an imported strain of rough-coated miniature dachshund, to bolt or dig to these 10lb rodents as traditional terriers, even some of the Devonshire terriers I saw advertised in 1963 are a bit big to get to ground. The indigenous Shelburne terrier – a puzzle to me, I'm no terrier expert – is too big, so Teddy goes out of her way to buy in good, working, rough-haired, miniature dachshunds.

She wrote to Plummer several times after she obtained his addresss from John Winch at Crufts, but Plummer never replied. In fact, in nearly 20 years I've never known him answer a letter. Even bills are written out by various women who occupy his life for a week or so, or simply by girls he teaches. I've never seen him write a letter or reply to a query except to scribble 10 or 12 words on the bottom of the sender's letter and return it. Eventually, I believe he sent her a tape to come and see him in England when she was next over here and true to her word Teddy turned up for one of Plummer's super rat hunts.

Next day Plummer took Teddy and I to the fells to get data for his book *Fell Terriers*. I feel just a bit treacherous about writing about Brian's peculiarities, but at an interview he doesn't take notes, he goes into a deep trance-like sleep, afterwards waking and remembering all the data word for word. It is nearly impossible to wake him from these near comatose conditions which sometimes start when we are driving on the motorway and he will say, 'Take over, David, I've an idea,' and is unconscious in a matter of seconds. This happened after an interview in Patterdale and much to Teddy's amazement he went into the

85

Teddy Moritz at the Coniston Hunt kennels.

traditional coma, leaving me to entertain Teddy, and Teddy to comment that Plummer really belonged on the set of *Star Trek*, which amused Plummer somewhat when he awoke four hours later and wrote up word for word his interview with an almost frightening accuracy.

Teddy kept up regular correspondence with Joan and I and visited us each time she came to Britain. Lurchers, or dogs by that name are unknown in America, though greyhounds with a dash of deerhound, wolfhound and even foxhound and pit bull are regularly bred for coyote and even wolf hunting and are run from the back of a well-sprung pick-up truck and are referred to as cold-blooded hounds – don't ask why, I just don't know. Collie lurchers are, however, unknown for some reason as are Bedlington crosses and suchlike. Teddy saw Romulus, watched him perform, was totally sold on him and asked for a puppy.

We mated Merle to a fine big greyhound and the bitch whelped a long-backed, sooty merle with a good type and strong feet. We ran it on, socialised it for her and sent it across on the plane. Teddy began work on it next day and before its first season she was drawing ground hogs, catching rabbits and showing what was likely to be an unfortunate interest in deer. She killed a raccoon or two for Teddy and looked like becoming her beau ideal of a dog. Scarcely a week went by without a photograph plus letter showing Teddy with a host of strange creatures and half a dozen rabbits on the back of her trailer. Her last letter was not so pleasant. Her bitch had run the scent of a deer and tracked it maybe a mile or so before Teddy, with dachshunds to ground, had noticed her missing. Teddy had run disconsolately through the woods only to find that the dog and deer had crossed a busy highway and the rest is easy for the reader to guess. Fortunately the bitch had been killed instantly, though the term 'fortunately' seems strangely out of place when any dog becomes a road casualty. The loss of the bitch left a huge gap in Teddy's life and as Merle was no longer at stud the chance of breeding a replacement was remote – though breeding any two merles which are duplicates is remote, even if one uses the same sire and the same dam to breed them.

Curiously, a duplicate, or near duplicate, was born about a month afterwards, a sooty merle of the same colour type and roughly the same marking was born in a litter sired by Taffy out of a bitch from the much-used sire Hardly Ever, an excellent greyhound and one whose 'breed' fits in quite nicely with the line I breed.

Teddy jumped at the chance of the puppy and a fortuitous choice it was to be. We ran the puppy on for about 14 weeks inoculating it against seemingly every transatlantic ill including rabies, thank God unknown here at the time of writing, but a problem in some states in the USA wherever bears, wolves, coyotes, foxes and mustelids abound. Exporting a puppy is really a bind and not at all the lucrative business some people would have the reader think. A suitable cage has to be constructed and officials of various varieties can deem the case suitable or unsuitable according to the way they've got out of bed that morning, and the dog has to be taken to Manchester Airport to fly out. Take into account the food, time spent socialising, transport fuss and bother and exporting a dog ceases to become a prestigious matter over which one can boast, but a costly, time-consuming bind and frankly very few people finish up in pocket after a transatlantic sale. However, Teddy is an exception to any rule and as a family we took to her instantly, hence nothing was too much trouble for us to help her.

Teddy with two white tailed jack rabbits caught by her blue merle lurcher Lee.

Teddy's puppy came on in leaps and bounds as she recorded a series of catches ranging from cotton tails to marmots or ground hogs and finally raccoon, bolted by terriers from a flood drain – a popular hiding place for a raccoon and marked by Teddy's lurcher. Sufficient to say Teddy writes regularly to provide us with a host of tales which could never have taken place in a country the size of Britain. When Plummer finds the world getting on top of him, not an infrequent occurrence lately, he retreats to John O'Groats six hundred miles away. Teddy travels that distance to run jack rabbit, the super hare of the American prairies, and thinks nothing of it.

Her lurcher gained a fair reputation for work and a few more transatlantic sales followed, each as arduous and time-consuming as the last. Still, I suppose I get a tremendous kick knowing my dogs have run quarry in all parts of the world and the letters of appreciation are ample payment for the trouble of rearing, transporting and socialising the puppies.

Not all exports or rather promised exports are as rewarding, however. I've had several requests to sell dogs to Saudi Arabia or to the Trucial States. Most have admittedly been tentative enquiries, such as the request I received at my first and last visit to Crufts in 1982, a visit I made primarily to meet George Henry Long of the Lakeland Terrier Club for I have scarcely any interest in the varieties of dogs kept for show. However, in 1985 I received what I believed to be a concrete order from a British Colonel acting on behalf of some oil-rich Sheik who had not quite the faith in the saluki as had his ancestors and who wished for a pair of gay pied to white, tight-coated, three quarter breds. It would be a lie to say that I simply fetched a puppy out of the litter. It was an all important sale, one which could consolidate the breeder's reputation in that part of the world. Finally I produced his puppy and what a puppy it turned out to be. Romey Brough, the artist, on her way to an exhibition called to see it and remarked on its perfect symmetry, and with an artist's eye for the aesthetic, expressed a wish to own or at least paint such a dog. It had perfect feet, a tail in balance with its shape, a magnificent intelligent head and the bouncy will to live which literally tells the buyer the dog is a goer just asking to be tried out. My daughter Sally, my wife Joan, and several other friends spent hours socialising the puppy and I began to build a carefully constructed crate for the dog which was, so I was told, to be shipped out by private airline. Days before its departure I received a curt cancellation letter stating the Sheik had plumped for greyhounds. Plummer advised keeping the dog, it was a raving beauty, but I was woefully over-dogged and finally sold the puppy to a hunter lamper who is probably blissfully unaware of the 'dog that might have been'.

It's all part of the game I support but not all lurcher breeding is beer and skittles and I'm about to bare my soul a little for the reader – and there's quite a lot to bare about the next subject in hand.

—10—

Questions a Lurcher Breeder is Asked

I'VE KEPT LIVESTOCK and bred dogs practically, all my life yet to consider myself an expert on dogs in general and lurchers in particular, would be a bit conceited to say the least. Yet in spite of the fact that I quite openly confess that I am not an expert, I get asked many questions and normally I am always being asked to give talks on lurchers and lurcher breeding, so perhaps it might be good sound common sense to answer a few questions in print and jump the gun just a little regarding any future talks I may be asked to give.

So straight from the shoulder and slam bang into the most common question I am asked. The phone rings, usually late at night, and a rather upset voice asks, 'I've bought a fully trained, guaranteed lurcher (I'm not quite sure what guaranteed lurcher means) and it just won't retrieve and simply stands over its kill or dummy, what can I do?' Sadly and I seldom mince words hence the brevity of this book – the answer is nothing. Once a sight hound bred lurcher or longdog in particular has failed to retrieve its kill and also failed to retrace its training with a dummy, there isn't a damn thing anyone can do except hold onto the dog awhile and see if it mends its ways, which incidentally it invariably won't. Failing that, lamp it regularly and go to keep fit classes yourself as you are in for a hell of a lot of running to pick up both kill and dummy.

Second question, thrown quite a lot at one time but rarely these days for some reason or other. 'You sell your dogs for £80 a puppy don't you?' I answer, 'Yes', politely knowing what is to come. 'Well, I can get a good, trained lurcher from Charlie Armstrong for the same price'. Answer, given very politely, 'Then I suggest you go to Charlie and buy his lurcher, though you may pause to ask why he is selling it, good night', and I quietly put the phone down. It's a four-to-one bet I will get that very same person phone up in a few days to request a visit to book a puppy. He is not the lunatic type and after a pause he will realise the wisdom of the statement.

Harder still are the phone calls asking advice over what to mate to their bitch. I have several stud dogs all except Richard at public stud providing the customer adheres to my rules. I make no bones about it, even if I am on my beam-end financially – and even during the financial storm caused by the parvo virus problem – the rules are for everyone and no one but no one, is allowed to take liberties with them. So back to the phone call. A voice at the other end of the phone says, 'My bitch has come into season and I want to mate her to one of your stud dogs.' I catch my breath and say, 'Of what breeding is your bitch?' If it is largely longdog bred, deerhound, whippet, greyhound, saluki etc (though let's face it, most backyard breeders – it's not a derogatory expression – make up pedigrees as the mood takes them), then providing the bitch seems to be what it is reported to be, I advise accordingly but allow the breeder a chance to disagree with my opinion. If the bitch is a greyhound/Bedlington/whippet/borzoi/deerhound/collie/greyhound then I usually ask the breeder his age. If he is a youngster I gently put it to him that he may well be breeding yet another litter of puppies for the lurcher rescue society and suggest that if he wants another lurcher that he buys a puppy – no, not from me, I hate con tricks of this nature played on me and refuse to do it to others. I also explain the economics of rearing a litter of puppies to him and give him a day or so to think about it. If the voice is that of an older client I usually ask if he has a potential market for the puppies and suggest he works out the economics of the lurcher breeding game – though Heaven knows in 1985 it can scarcely be called a game.

Funnily enough, I am seldom plagued with lunatics of the sort that caused Phil Lloyd and Plummer to go ex-directory. I get some – Plummer has begged me to record them as data for books though he was singularly unenthusiastic about recording them himself I must add – and I've been tempted to do this at times but such an action makes enemies and I'd hate to be lampooned by Brian who has an adder-like tongue and transmits his venom to paper just as easily. Don't make enemies, try to be amicable and do your best not to upset anyone is the motto of the House of Hancock – though it's a bit of a hard rule to follow at times.

Next, I think it's about time that I explain why I attend only a few lurcher shows and refuse to judge either contests or shows. Once again let's be perfectly honest about the matter. Judges are seldom the most popular people in the world. They make three people happy and the rest of the show very embittered. My business is to sell lurchers to satisfied customers and such a business demands good will. If I make enemies I lose clients and if I judge shows I make enemies. It's as simple as that, a matter of pure economics and look at it this way, any manager of a Mothercare shop would be out of his mind to offer to judge a baby show. I think I have a good eye for conformation, I don't go in for dissection as Brian does, though secretly Plummer cannot even put down his own dogs, let alone dissect them – and haven't I knocked a man who regards me as one of his closest friends – but I can pick out a showy puppy as well as most. Show qualities don't really interest me though I have every admiration for Dave McNee who has some really nice show stock. I breed, or at least try to breed, honest-to-goodness work dogs and if one turns out to be a bobby-dazzler capable of picking up rosettes, so much the better. It gives the owner a pride in his dogs that will push him through sticky patches in training which often sour a lurcher owner and make him sell his dogs, but I don't breed for show nor do I tell the prospective buyer his puppy looks like a rosette gatherer.

I've always tried to be honest with future buyers and found it pays results a hundred times over. I don't make extravagant claims for my dogs and if someone wants a hare killer and nothing else I usually pass him on to someone who breeds a goodish sort of longdog preferably with a dash of saluki blood. If a man requests a Bedlington/whippet I don't try to sell him a collie lurcher but I keep a useful list of breeders of various crosses and pass the customer to the breeder. I hope they do the same to me – I think they do actually.

A typical litter record in the stud book.

I've taken to tattooing the ears of my dogs recently. It serves several purposes. First, I've met or rather been rung up by irate people who claim I've bred a dog which is a little less than useful (I don't advertise every one is a winner) only to find that the dog has changed hands so frequently that a pedigree unknown animal has become a Hancock special as a sales gimmick. I feel a little like putting brand labels on tins of peas tattooing the puppies, but it serves other purposes as well. I use a complex index system so I know which bitches throw goodish workers and which throw world-beaters – that's if I've ever bred a world-beater which I probably haven't. Next, it fascinates Plummer who will scan and memorise pages of notes in seconds – well, everyone should have an interest (sorry Brian!) – and he believes that somewhere in the vast morass of figures lies some scientific secret. So don't accept a Hancock puppy without a genuine Hancock brand mark on it folks. One without a complex ear tattoo is not one of mine, not since June 1985 when I decided to adopt this practice.

It's a curious fact that once a lurcher breeder has started up and become established he gets lots of offers of dubious puppies and in no time a reputable breeder of known stock becomes an out-and-out dealer with the typical dealer's reputation for shady deals and sales of puppies with fictitious pedigrees. I've been approached just once regarding such a transaction and I admit perhaps the puppies were what the vendor said they were. I turned down the offer flat and frankly, despite the fact that Brian has bred his family long enough for the batch to be termed a strain, I would even refrain from selling his stock. I've tried my hardest to breed only my particular type, and while I make no particular claim that stock I breed is the best in the world, they are the best I can produce and each year I try my best to breed stock a little better than I did the year before.

Funnily enough, I've taken to giving talks at The Forest Community Centre, Walsall, a centre which is now developing a good reputation for fieldsport speakers and amazing as it may seem I get many questions on animal photography from the audience assembled there. Up until a few years ago photography was an amateur passion – and I say amateur as while I won several awards for my work, I seldom sold a photograph nor went out of my way to do so. These days I get hosts of orders for photographs people have seen in various books I have illustrated. It's a time-consuming job developing and printing film and I live in a very time-consuming world so if the reader is of those who has had to wait for a beloved photograph he has ordered, all I can say is I'm sorry. There are 24 hours in every day and I seem to work most of those.

One tale to end a chapter – it's a good tale and a truthful one at that. Vermuiel of Stratford bought a lovely, wall-eyed, dun merle dog from me and was to say the least a bit disappointed. His dog was elegant, fast and a good worker, but it just didn't catch. The old adage, if at first you don't succeed try, try and try again, he took in his stride, but it became

Vermuiel's red merle.

just a bit obvious that the young man was not exactly relishing his lack of success. Timmy and Romulus, contemporaries of Vermuiel's dog, were coming on in leaps and bounds. Vermuiel's dog was not. For a while I considered offering him his money back though I was aware that while the boy was disappointed he really loved and cared for his dog, which shone like glass and was as hard as rock. He came to our farm regularly, each time more down in the mouth and I resisted the temptation of showing him photographs of Timmy and Romulus' kills. Well, autumn came and Vermuiel turned up at the farm quietly smug with a Cheshire cat look on his usually slightly sad face. He reached three hares out of his van and put them down on our concrete path. His dog had killed all three one afternoon, and has not looked back since. I wish to goodness the owners of 'for sale' and 'free to good home' lurchers or contributors to lurcher rescue societies would give their dogs the same chance and I often wonder if half the poor devils given the same chance as Vermuiel's lurcher would have made it.

—11—

The Coming of Parvo Virus

PLUMMER STATES THAT he is about a year in front of every veterinary surgeon in the UK disease wise. He has college friends in most of the animal research labs and probably obtains prior and a bit illegal information about diseases before most vets get view of it. In 1976 he lost a litter of Jack Russell terriers to a disease suddenly and totally. They were fine at ten weeks and dead two days later. The pathology report revealed nothing untoward and he entered the cause of death as 'unknown enteritis' in his November 14th diary entry. He bred rarely at that time as he was plagued with thefts and bred first-rate terriers for his and his use only, so the nasty bug which had a chance to die off didn't appear again until 1981, when it once again appeared in the Midlands.

Brian always blames himself for bringing parvo to my premises and is forever apologising for it. Personally I don't think it could have been avoided. His line of Jack Russell terrier had run thin and so he bought a black Fell terrier called Nightwing to introduce to his strain. Predominantly Brian Nuttall bred, she was an eye-catcher and just about the right size for the job. Two weeks later she went down with very debilitating enteritis, an enteritis which dehydrated her body and caused her to look ill. Plummer dosed her with Nuvamide, then the panacea for the disease of stomach and gut, gave her sips of an electrolyte solution – half a spoonful every half-hour – and she recovered, or appeared to as she went down with another similar bout weeks later.

He lost an odd puppy or so in the occasional litter for a month, sent away a specimen to Glasgow Veternary Research Laboratories and by then I think he was well aware of the cause of the disease. It did him very little damage, he seldom bred, never sold to buyers and had no one to the house he didn't expressly invite. My own lot was just a shade different. I had just produced my first top-grade lurchers and was getting into the swing of breeding puppies of good class and with regularity. An attack of parvo virus is in fact one of the worst things that can happen to a breeder just about to leave the 'traps' to become a recognised breeder of good-class stock. The trouble was, and this is ironic, that the genetic mix I was putting together, particularly the silky three quarter breds, were as good as I could breed. The half bred, crop-trained to a good standard, was receiving excellent reports from people. The Warrener of *Shooting News* was over the moon with delight at the puppy he was training.

The outbreak of parvo set the clock back a year or so and that was at the very barest minimum. We lost puppies at varying ages which looked as right as rain in the morning and were dead by nightime. If my wife Joan – God bless her inbred sense of stockmanship – saw a slightly unhappy puppy we took it in the house in a tea chest, put a heat lamp on it, dosed it hourly with an electrolyte solution called Lectade, specifically designed for pigs and calves, but also suitable for dogs if diluted down enough, and quite a few recovered. Quite a few didn't, however, and though Joan often worked the trick with ailing puppies, we buried many which had required a lot of hard work rearing them and had been given lots of love and affection by both Sally and Joan.

We set to with a vengeance, bleaching floors with hypochlorite solution (the sort that kills all known germs, dead), scrubbed the brick walls of whelping pens, and just about suffocated ourselves on chlorine gas given off from the action of the hypochlorite on the chemicals in the concrete and for a litter or two we checked the spread, but it returned again three months later despite the fact we worked like dogs and vaccinated every puppy with the dead virus vaccine which was then available.

It was bad enough losing puppies at home, worse still telling clients who had picked puppies their animals had died, but a hundred times worse telling people who had bought puppies and had them die that we were 'very sorry'. Refunding their money just didn't seem enough after people had lavished care and training on a pup only to have it die the horrible death one associates with parvo virus. I'd get frantic phone calls from owners of stricken puppies who wanted help, but what the Dickens could I say or do. The puppies invariably died and I refunded the money. My food bill was £80 a week at one point – and I was struggling to pay it, but I had no puppies to sell and no income apart from the seed and plant trade Joan and I had drummed up with my growing plants and Joan working 16 hours a day on market stalls. I put down puppies which even looked a bit off-colour and if a badly infected puppy recovered I dared not sell it because of the possibility of damage to its heart, damage which would manifest itself a year or so later when the whelp simply keeled over and died.

True, we had spells when parvo didn't hit us – usually in mid-winter, but then we'd get whole litters going down with the dreaded bug and there just didn't seem to be an answer. Plummer put the whole pile of data I collected through a computer, stayed up nights collecting results and came back baffled and usually in a really bad depression due to his failure. My vet came up with no answer either, though he's a straight out of college, bang up to date sort of chap who follows every development regarding canine disease. Things always look blackest before the dawn, so the saying goes, but this dawn seemed to be a hell of a long time coming and frankly I couldn't see any light at the end of the tunnel.

Well, light did eventually begin to dawn and Plummer and I came up with the answer at possibly just about the same time, though a few college friends had heard of a new live vaccine which was receiving good reports. A firm called Intervet had produced a brand new vaccine named Novi-Vac-Parvo-C for which the firm made fairly extravagant claims. Injected at four weeks the vaccine over-ran the bitch's natural immunity given to the litter by the collustrum and gave the puppy immunity to 12 weeks. The puppies, however, needed to be reared in disease-free kennels so I moved my batch of puppies around a little, rearing them in outlandish places well away from my tailor-made whelping pens. I then obtained the vaccine and did every puppy. It was a long shot, a very long shot, and I reckon the chances were a bit remote to say the least, but on reflection and judging from my past record which was anything but spectacular then, what in the name of Heaven had I to lose?

I followed my vet's advice to the letter. Whelping the litter in the now very strongly disinfected, but still very infected whelping sheds, moving them off heat at 10 days to new quarters still on the farm and injecting at four weeks of age. Meanwhile Brian had deliberately bred a litter of white German shepherd puppies to test out the vaccine under a slightly different control group method to see if a breakthrough could be made. He steam-cleaned a shed and fumigated with formaldehyde (formaldehyde and chlorine are the only two easily obtained chemicals which can cope with a virus whereas most disinfectants kill bacteria). I have a lot to thank for the training I received while rearing poultry which are regular havens for all the diseases under the sun.

Well, we sat back and waited. Plummer at his premises, me at mine, phoning each day to exchange notes but staying well clear of each other's premises lest there should be the remote – and it must have been remote – chance of cross hybridisation. The weeks dragged by with Plummer more worried than I was for he had applied for a grant to breed guide dogs for the blind in Scotland and had pledged his cottage to fund the project. Frankly, and this isn't meant to hurt, Plummer is a bit of an unsuitable stock breeder who takes the death of every puppy to heart and becomes ill if a litter teeters on death's door. A stock breeder must harden his heart when things go wrong, as they invariably do and while he must strive like mad to keep his stock alive he must shrug off death philosophically. Brian just can't do this. He is basically a hunter, a geneticist, a first-rate student of dog behaviour and an expert on dog lore. He is not the stuff of which stock breeders are made and I fear his Scottish venture is doomed to failure as gloom follows his first real set back. One more derogatory comment about a best friend. He has to my knowledge not sold dogs and would be ill at ease doing so. How he will manage in Scotland baffles me, though I wish him all the luck he has always wished me.

Weeks passed and no sign of parvo appeared. I think when one expects the outbreak of a disease every little disorder becomes a manifestation of the illness and the breeder, even the normal breeder, develops a form of paranoia. Every weepy eye caused by a straw poking a puppy in the eye was a parvo sign and we waited with baited breath for it to show. A puppy with an off-day, when it was just a bit off-colour, became a parvo victim, but as the days ticked by I found no trace of parvo virus and not a sign of the red muccus-ridden droppings one associates with a parvo 'dier'. The vaccine makers had made seemingly wild claims of these products. Now the proof of the pudding was clearly in the eating and as no more puppies even looked off-colour we began to develop faith in the vaccine providing – and this is a big proviso – the maker's instructions are carried out to the letter and the litter is moved to a clean disinfected pen where the challenge of the virus is not allowed to test the vaccine too soon. I think we have won, not as Brian would like as a clean KO, but more of a points victory for I now inject all puppies for parvo virus and also for distemper, hard pad, hepatitis and leptospiroris before sale. True, the increased price of a puppy may put off a few buyers – well, tough luck I say. I'm in business to breed what I hope to be good lurchers and I just can't afford another setback which frankly put me back on my haunches and made me wonder what the heck I was doing breeding lurchers and perhaps I should just run a small team of lurchers and get my kicks out of lamping, photography and a spot of daytime coursing.

I'm in the lurcher breeding business. I breed the best I can – I don't make extravagant claims – it's a bit stupid to do so, but equally I can't afford set backs which decimate (wrong word, Plummer tells me decimate means kills one in ten and I've hit worse patches than that). My dream, my ambition, is to produce 100% satisfied customers and supply them with 100% healthy puppies. I think – oh God, I hope I'm over the rough patch – but I've told the reader the truth the whole truth and nothing but the truth. Seemingly no writer ever experiences a mishap, a problem, a tribulation, or an outbreak of disease – or at least they never say so. I have, and I doubt if I'm out of the wood even now, for in dog breeding there is bound to be another problem just lurking around the corner.

—12—

On a More Controversial Note

I THINK ANYONE who starts out on the road to lurcher keeping must obviously be aware that it's not all fun and anyone who doesn't aquaint himself with the problems he is likely to face is not only a fool, but heading for a series of very miserable disappointments.

One of the advantages of breeding from greyhound brood bitches, and there are many believe me, is that providing one goes to a reputable

A good quality coursing greyhound. Note the strong front legs.

breeder of good quality coursing stock then you can bet that the dogs are not only in fine fettle but have been inoculated and boosted so regularly that there is literally no danger of the animals succumbing to any of the common diseases such as distemper, hard pad, hepatitis and leptospirosis. So far then it's a home run and quite clearly the greyhound bitch is the obvious starting point for the lurcher breeder.

My niece Lucy who, when she visits us, spends all day with Old Sally.

However, stop a moment for not everything in every garden is lovely. Greyhounds are capricious creatures, and while I have never ever seen and certainly never owned a greyhound which was in any way nasty with even the smallest child – my nieces and nephews inflict awful torment on some of my best broods only to be greeted with wags of tails and forlorn looks when the torture stops and we take the child away – they can never really be trusted with each other and certainly not with smaller kennel mates. A terrier fight – we bred a few Fells and Russells – can usually be sensed almost as one senses a storm building up, but greyhound battles break out with startling suddenness and for no apparent reason although feeding time is as good as any reason for a pitched battle. Don't under any circumstances underrate the rather frail-looking jaws of a greyhound and the apparent total absence of the powerful biting muscles which characterise bull terriers. A bite from a greyhound is something to remember. It is policy to stay with greyhounds while they feed and make sure no angry scenes are brewing. Once fed, they seldom fight except over a bone or something else vaguely edible, but a fight will invariably result in a really bad tear in the skin and a trip to the vet is almost a certainty. Greyhounds can be damnably fickle – bitches reared together from the nest sometimes let loose on each other with a madness that makes the onlooker think that they have always been mortal enemies. Trust them all you like, but always treat their biting powers with the greatest respect. Once cat and stock broken no animal makes a more delightful house pet. They are fastidiously clean, moult little and have endearing dispositions completely free of guile, viciousness, and even if stepped on accidentally never ever retaliate. Then one day an incident will occur and hey ho, they up and kill a pet terrier with whom they have shared the same basket for years. Every breed of dog has its faults, Alsatians (I hate the term German shepherd dogs) are apt to be a little overkeen to guard, terriers are snappy, spaniels are slobbery, greyhounds are not to be trusted with other dogs of the same sex.

Visitors to my kennels are my life blood – they bring me trade and allow my business to prosper. They are also bringers of disease and I am aware I run the gauntlet of an epidemic every time visitors come to my kennels. It's hard to pick out a disease-carrying dog unless it is examined carefully and it's impossible to be able to tell a man whose clothes carry the deadly distemper virus. Usually a general light-hearted conversation on the phone – questions about how many dogs the man has, how his last lurcher died, does he bother to inoculate – will alert the buyer as quickly as a red traffic light. A chap who has had a lurcher die suddenly after a fit is a biological time bomb and it is as well to advise him to wait three months before buying another puppy. The

A visitor being shown a litter by my daughter Sally.

chances are he won't and he will visit some other person, demand to buy a puppy and wipe out his kennels while he is doing it.

Greyhounds are not the only trials and tribulations I have to put up with. A person visiting my farm may be greeted by a host of free-running stud dogs ranging from pure bred collies to three quarter breds like the fast-ageing Romulus and Timmy. Many question, 'Do you work all of them?' To say yes would not only be a downright lie but obviously ludicrous. Each dog is given a try to prove its worth and only worked lightly after that. True Timmy, Romulus and Monty have taken a bit of a bashing and it's beginning to show, but once Taffy's worth as a stud was established only a lunatic runs a dog which can breed such puppies. He was retired as soon as he became a proficient catch dog and has seldom been 'out' since. I simply can't afford to lose such a dog.

Likewise the collies. Richard is tied or penned up but Remus simply refuses to be kept on a tether. Hence I have a few underworked lurchers being constantly baited by a very underworked collie, which herded Joan's goats to distraction and drove just about every chicken on the farm nuts by constantly gathering them up. Fights are inevitable and invariably the collies are in the thick of it. They could be prevented by kennelling them separately, but a collie needs liberty to develop mentally and annoying as Remus is, quite a lot of his character would be lost if he was chained or confined. Such deterioration in character can not be passed on to this progeny but to confine him now would be a little like clipping the wings on a peregrine falcon. He has come unstuck recently when he irritated three free-running lurchers and he became embroiled in a fight which nearly killed him. This made me realise that the dog which is a valuable stud dog throwing level, rough-coated deerhound-type puppies, elegant but very hard-wearing, was going to be hard to replace and I took Brian's offer of a bearded collie puppy to replace Remus should he fall off the constant tightrope he is walking by irritating dogs five and six times his size.

My new beardie will be bred in the purple out of a Dunsyre bred bitch – fully trained and well capable of turning a black-faced ram – mated to the famous Paul Turnbull's Blue, reckoned by many to be the finest bearded collie in the country. Blue, a tall, elegant dog, may well be one of the dogs mentioned by Logan who believes the merest dash or so of deerhound blood was added several hundred years ago to bring

Visitors with Sally being greeted by a host of dogs.

the beardie up on the leg, to be able to work the precipitous-sided hills around Dumfries. Certainly Blue is a magnificent animal, as large as Taffy with both leg and substance – the ideal dog for a first cross for all round work. Blue's parents bred at the birthplace of the pirate John Paul Jones in Dumfries, are also tall, leggy dogs – though Moorland,

Remus rushes up to a billy goat and carefully avoids the stamp and the horns.

the founder of the strain, was a shepherd around the high country near Glasgow before he became settled in Kirkbean. Replacement studs are absolutely essential in a properly run kennel and without them the breeder resorts to the odds and sods breeding and his reputation goes out of the window. It is a private joke between Plummer and myself that because he is gathering a family of top class bearded collies together to breed a kennel of this renowned working dog, that I will get to know the A9 (the road to John O'Groats), but I think that in spite of the extra stock I am having to carry I shall breed my own small strain of working beardies and Plummer may well have to know the A38 to find suitable studs for his own kennels! As I've said it's a private joke and one the reader may not appreciate or understand.

I suppose I've lost remarkably few greyhounds through fighting though I've picked up more than a fair share of vet's bills because of bickering and minor skirmishing. A really aggressive greyhound is a killer and as much a headache as anyone could desire and there is usually only one place for such an animal – the least said the better from here on I'm afraid. Furthermore, a really bad fighter, the sort of screamer who goes into hysterics every time another dog large or small passes near, seems to infect the whole kennel with its madness and crazy fights. Really outrageous battles take place in calm and placid greyhound stables as soon as a lunatic is introduced into their midst. I watch greyhounds carefully before adding them to my kennels and I reject out of hand anything that is for the want of a better expression – slightly loopy. Loopy greyhounds are not common, thank God, though track fighters are always a bit suspect. However, track fighting is

My new beardie Brian – Turnbull's Blue × Plummer's Dot.

107

probably due to the state of near hysteria generated by the sound of the electric hare coming around and some trainers actually believe that once a dog has steadied – gone out of the crazy stage – they revert to normal and simply chase the hare. However, the working life of a greyhound is so short there usually isn't time to get the dog out of this crazy stage and thus the majority of track fighters usually finish up the way of all flesh so to speak. I don't like them and while I admit I've had a few and bred quite a few puppies of note from one in particular, I go for the steady greyhound for preference every time. They are less trouble to manage, less trouble to feed, no trouble to kennel and the lurcher breeder realises that a retired dog of this calibre has given of its best and deserves a place in kennels rather than a visit to the maggot factory. I don't like greyhounds with bad feet all that much either. Weak tarsals, carpals and wrists which don't hold up well on a well-smoothed cinder track aren't exactly likely to be good qualities to pass on to lurchers which are likely to be run over country where a mountain goat would have a rather bad time.

Some time ago, December 1985 I think, some chap wrote into *Shooting News* with a comment that the very worst whippet/greyhound would be better than the very best collie/greyhound ever born. Well, to deny any chap the right of free speech would be unfair and unwise as well as I've seen quite a few useful whippet/greyhounds – Joan, my wife, reared a litter for Brian during his experimental years, I think it would be around 1970 or perhaps a year or so before. Quite a few made handy dogs – one or two didn't as I think Plummer would be the first to admit, but the majority would have been classed as good honest workers. I think most suffered foot injuries if run over bad country and fewer still had a long and productive life as lampers and grafting dogs. I think the ones I breed, both the half breds and to a certain extent even the fine-boned three quarter breds, would have a longer life on the field and one or two of the three quarter breds put up a goodish sort of show on the lurcher races against whippet/greyhounds. However, as it's every man to his taste and because I don't breed this cross it would be madness to condemn the hybrid. If the chap likes them then the best of luck to him and it's a big world so long may he prosper. Not everyone wants the same sort of animal and as a classic example I'll knock poor old Brian again who has taken much flack throughout this book. He breeds a very mongrelly – they breed true to type actually – strain of lurcher and adds large dashes of collie blood every generation, so much so in fact that I've seen almost pure border collies appear in his litters. My brother-in-law, Cyril, has one of this family and it serves him well and certainly adapts to Plummer's needs. They are fast off the mark, quick to pick up and are excellent catch dogs and suit Plummer down to

Plummer with his excellent bitch Fathom.

the ground. My own are a different kettle of fish and have greater stamina and just as much poke, and my three quarter breds are a great deal faster. If the man who wrote the condemnation of the collie hybrid wanted a literary argument, as my bet is he did, then I'm sorry but what is one man's meat is another man's poison. I've reared, bred and trained longdogs of whippet, greyhound, deerhound and saluki types

109

and even kept a borzoi. Fine, they suit a lot of people who would have no other crosses. They just don't suit me.

My brother-in-law's lurcher Whitey (Merle × Fathom) handled by his son David.

—13—

The Future

I
T'S A WISE man who can predict what the future holds and I
make no pretence at being clever, let alone wise. I've weathered a
few rough patches in my life and I have no illusions there are more
ahead of me.

The fashions in lurchers change dramatically. Once the *Exchange and
Mart*, a good paper for lurchers though I seldom advertise in it, only
carried deerhound hybrids for sale, now scarcely a deerhound/
greyhound hybrid is advertised. Perhaps the collie lurcher too will go
out of fashion, though I hope not as I'm afraid I'm stuck with the cross.
As I've said they suit me down to the ground and while it would be a
downright lie to say they suit everyone and that I never get a dis-
gruntled customer, they may not be the best in the world but they're the
best I can breed so I'll continue no matter how the fashions change. I

*A beardie/border collie/greyhound hybrid (¼ greyhound, ¾ collie) named Enock
at 8 months old.*

may vary the breeding of my studs – no, hold on – I mean I'll change the collie and maybe the greyhound but the basic cross will be the same, and I may produce a distinct set of lines of bearded collie and border collie hybrid. I still like merles I admit but colour isn't really important in lurchers except to the client that is, and once again the client is always right – providing they don't ask me to breed exotic or different crosses – as I've explained I've learned my lesson the hard way.

Katie a yellow eyed red Dartmoor collie.

I'll probably keep a few bearded stud dogs as well as the odd half bred stud dogs and as Plummer is going in for breeding beardies in a big way and buying in the very best working blood in Britain in case the breed gets extinct, I'll have no trouble in getting exactly what I want.

I mated old Sally, a skeletal veteran too useful and too beloved to put down, to Richard last year and bred a Taffy look-alike. Taffy was an ugly brute as a puppy, high on the hind quarters, low-fronted and generally not at all shapely, until one day I looked up and found my ugly duckling – and he was ugly – had become a beautiful swan. His brother, a duplicate, has grown apace and at 10 months is a large silky-coated merle, and if I'm asked if I've bred a better half bred the

Bonnie and Clyde, Katie's son and daughter by Chuck Arrowsmith's collie Gyp.

answer is no, I haven't. He's a joy to look at and moves like a Morgan three quarter bred horse. I'm experimenting with Dartmoor collies next year. It's a trial run so I'll say no more. Enough to say they are a bit hardier, taller, rangier than the border collie, but until I've tested the line and it's progeny it's a bit foolish to say any more than that. I might be predicting success and the end product a howling failure. I hope the cross is a step forward. If it isn't, then back to the drawing board and scrap the line. It sounds hard but it's the only way with stock breeding.

I break with Brian this year – I think neither of us likes the prospect. He had a coronary in June 1985 – Joan predicted nearly the day – and I think he's hankering for medical discharge from teaching for he teaches in a really rough area of Walsall. Chances are he'll sell up and hightail it to John O'Groats. I spent autumn at his cottage with Phil Lloyd and loved it, but it's a lonely place. He won't have a telephone installed so perhaps he'll really learn what isolation means. How we'll keep in touch is a problem as I don't think Brian is capable of writing a letter unless it's an attack on some local bigwig or other. If he dies he's promised to let me know – work that one out, I can't – but the chances are that one day I'll pull up at a long-distance cafe and find a Thurso fish wagon with a mass of genetic squiggles written on the dust of the side together with a few calculations and calculus symbols and I'll know he's still with us. He says he intends to cut himself off from the world in general and he believes that one day he'll come South to find to his surprise, the country devastated by atomic war. However, I doubt if we'll lose touch. We've been friends for too long and having written this I suddenly find I've run out of things to say.

Plummer's lonely cottage with Monty and Chuckles in the foreground.